THE INTERPRETATION OF
FINANCIAL STATEMENTS

The Interpretation

of

Financial Statements

BY

BENJAMIN GRAHAM

AND

CHARLES McGOLRICK

*A third revision of the book by
Benjamin Graham and Spencer B. Meredith
first published in 1937*

HARPER & ROW, PUBLISHERS
New York, Hagerstown, San Francisco, London

Library of Congress Cataloging in Publication Data

Graham, Benjamin, 1894-
    The interpretation of financial statements.
    "A third revision of the book of Benjamin Graham and
Spencer B. Meredith, first published in 1937."
    1. Financial statements.   I. McGolrick, Charles,
joint author.   II. Title.
HG4028.B2G7   1975   657'.3   74-15829
ISBN 0-06-011566-1

81 82 83 84 10 9 8 7 6

CONTENTS

Preface

This book is designed to enable you to read financial statements intelligently. Financial statements are intended to give an accurate picture of a company's condition and operating results, in a condensed form. Everyone who comes in contact with corporations and their securities has occasion to read balance sheets and income statements. Every businessman and investor is expected to be able to understand these corporation statements. For security salesmen and for customers' brokers in particular, the ability to analyze statements is essential. When you know what the figures mean, you have a sound basis for good business judgment.

Our plan of procedure is to deal successively with the elements that enter into the typical balance sheet and income account. We intend first to make clear what is meant by the particular term or expression, and then to comment briefly upon its significance in the general picture. Wherever possible we shall suggest simple standards or tests which the investor may use to determine whether a company's showing in a given respect is favorable or the reverse. Much of this material may appear rather elementary, but even in the elementary aspects of the subject there are peculiarities and pitfalls which it is important to recognize and guard against.

Of course the success of an investment depends ultimately upon future developments, and the future may never be "analyzed" with accuracy. But if you have precise information as to a company's present financial position and its past earnings record, you are better equipped to gauge its future possibilities. And this is the essential function and value of security analysis.

The material in this book is designed either for independent study as an elementary work or as an introduction to a more detailed treatment of the subject—such as *Security Analysis* by Ben-

vii

jamin Graham, David L. Dodd, and Sidney Cottle (McGraw-Hill, 1962). In the present revised edition, the treatment and the illustrations have been brought up to date.

Considerable use is made of the composite financial reports of United States manufacturing corporations, published jointly by the Federal Trade Commission and the Securities and Exchange Commission.

B. G.
C. McG.

New York City
November 1, 1974

1

Financial Statements in General

A full financial statement contains two major parts: an income account and a balance sheet. The income account shows the earnings for the period covered, while the balance sheet sets forth "the financial position" at the closing date. The company's report may include additional statements and supplementary schedules, such as an analysis of changes in capital and surplus, a summary of the "cash flow," and others.

The annual report is issued as of the close of the company's fiscal year. In the majority of cases this is December 31, but a large number of businesses select some other date. This would generally be after the close of the active season, when inventories and current liabilities are likely to be at a low point.

In addition to the annual report, nearly all concerns issue interim statements, usually containing the earnings only, but sometimes including the balance sheet as well. Monthly figures are available for all railroads and most public utilities. Other businesses—referred to for convenience as "industrials"—for the most part publish their results quarterly.

2

Balance Sheets in General

A balance sheet shows how a company stands at a given moment. There is no such thing as a balance sheet covering the year 1973; it can be for only a single date, for example, December 31, 1973. A single balance sheet may give some indications as to the company's past performance, but this may be studied intelligently only in the income accounts and by a comparison of successive balance sheets.

The function of the balance sheet is to show what the company owns and what it owes. In the form of the balance sheet now in general use all the items owned are listed in a left column and called the assets. The liabilities—what the company owes—are listed in a column to the right.

The assets include money the company holds or has invested, money owed to it by others, and the physical properties. Sometimes there are also intangible assets, now representing chiefly the price paid for acquisitions above the original cost of the tangible assets bought.

The liability side lists all the debts of the corporation and the equity or ownership interest of the stockholders. Debts incurred in the operation of the business appear as accounts payable. The more formal borrowings are listed as bonds or notes outstanding. Reserves of various kinds may also be listed as liabilities.

The stockholders' interest is called capital and surplus. These are liabilities only in the sense that they represent the amount for which the company is responsible to the stockholders. More truly, they are the arithmetical difference between the assets and the

2

liabilities, and they are placed among the liabilities to bring the balance sheet into balance. A balance sheet in the typical form:

Assets	$5,000,000	Liabilities	$4,000,000
		Capital & surplus	1,000,000
	$5,000,000		$5,000,000

really means:

Assets	$5,000,000
Less liabilities	4,000,000
Stockholders' interest	$1,000,000

The balance sheet presented below is taken from the financial reports published quarterly by the Federal Trade Commission and the Securities and Exchange Commission covering United States manufacturing corporations. It shows the combined assets and liabilities of a large sampling of companies at the end of 1973.

New and more informative methods of presentation of the bal-

TABLE 1
U.S. MANUFACTURING CORPORATIONS
BALANCE SHEET
December 31, 1973
(millions of dollars)

ASSETS		LIABILITIES & STOCKHOLDERS' EQUITY		
Cash & equivalent	$ 44,490	Short-term loans		$ 31,211
Accounts receivable	139,342	Accounts payable		75,801
Inventories	170,875	Income taxes accrued		17,069
Other current assets	31,314	Other current liabilities		71,890
Total current assets	386,021	Total current liabilities		195,971
Property, plant &		Long-term loans & debt		126,747
equipment	529,091			
Less reserve for de-		Other noncurrent liabilities		33,166
preciation & depletion	250,698			
Net property plant &				
equipment	278,393	Total		355,884
Other noncurrent assets	77,852	Capital	120,387	
		Surplus	265,996	
		Stockholders' equity		386,383
Total assets	$742,266	Total liabilities		$742,266

ance sheet are gradually becoming popular in corporate statements. The annual report of the U.S. Steel Corporation presents the information as a Statement of Financial Position. This is a single column of figures which arrives at the stockholders' investment by deducting the liabilities from the assets.

TABLE 2

UNITED STATES STEEL CORPORATION
CONSOLIDATED STATEMENT OF FINANCIAL POSITION
December 31, 1973

Current assets	
Cash	$ 252,785,694
Marketable securities	310,119,523
Receivables	795,415,400
Inventories	629,132,338
Total	$1,987,452,955
Less	
Current liabilities	
Notes & accounts payable	$ 573,031,368
Employment costs	449,564,891
Accrued taxes	340,490,998
Dividends payable	27,083,869
Debt due within one year	14,407,995
Total	$1,404,579,121
Working capital	$ 582,873,834
Plant replacement fund	255,000,000
Miscellaneous investments	71,795,777
Long-term receivables	261,510,077
Plant & equipment net	4,209,777,493
Operating parts & supplies	58,196,935
Costs applicable to the future	74,801,414
Total assets less current liabilities	$5,513,955,530
Deduct	
Long-term debt	$1,420,312,767
Reserves	100,276,769
Deferred taxes on income	182,210,627
Excess of assets over liabilities & reserves	$3,811,155,367
Ownership evidenced by	
Common stock	$1,625,083,860
Income reinvested in the business	2,186,071,507
Total	$3,811,155,367

We believe that the company's presentation could be improved from the viewpoint of analysts and investors by the following changes:

1. Include the plant replacement fund in current assets. The segregation of the assets is an arbitrary choice by the management, and it makes the working capital position appear weaker than it actually is.

2. The plant and equipment account should be stated thus:

Gross plant and equipment	$10,398 million	
Less depreciation and depletion	6,188　　"	
Plant and equipment net		$4,210 million

3

Total Assets and Total Liabilities

The totals of assets and liabilities appearing on the balance sheet supply a rough indication of the size of the company. Years ago it was customary to inflate the assets by including a large amount of fictitious "good will," either as a separate item or by merely including it with the property account. This practice is now all but extinct. To some extent the contrary situation prevails today, since in many cases the property-account figure shown on the statement is far below its current replacement value. It is also true that many companies possess valuable patents, trademarks, and ordinary good will which are not reflected in the asset account.

The size of a company may be measured in terms either of its assets or of its sales. In both cases the significance of the figure is entirely relative, and must be judged against the background of the industry. The assets of a small railroad will exceed those of a good-sized department store. From the investment standpoint, especially that of the buyer of high-grade bonds or preferred stocks, it may be well to attach considerable importance to large size. This would be true particularly in the case of industrial companies, for in this field the smaller enterprise is more subject to sudden adversity than is likely in a railroad or public utility. Where the purchase is made for speculative profit, or long-term capital gains, it is not so essential to insist upon dominant size, for there are countless examples of smaller companies prospering more than large ones. After all, the large companies themselves presented the best speculative opportunities, and perhaps investment opportunities as well, while they were still comparatively small.

6

4

Capital and Surplus

The interest or equity of the stockholders in the business, as shown by the books, is represented by capital and surplus. In the typical case, the money paid in by the stockholders is designated as capital, and the profits not paid out as dividends make up the surplus (or "reinvested earnings"). The capital is represented by shares of stock, sometimes of only one kind or class, sometimes of various kinds, which are usually called preferred and common. Other titles have also come into use, such as Class A or Class B, deferred shares, founders' shares, etc. The rights and limitations of various kinds of stock cannot safely be inferred from their title, but the facts must be definitely ascertained from the charter provisions, which in turn are summarized in the investors' manuals or other statistical records and reference books.

The shares may be either of a definite par value or without par. In the simple case the par value shows how much capital was paid in for each share by the original subscribers to the stock. A company with one million shares, par $100, would presumably represent a far greater investment than another company with one million shares, par $5. However, in the modern corporate setup neither the par value nor the total dollar value of the capital stock may be in the slightest degree informing. The capital figure is frequently stated at much less than the actual amount paid in by the stockholders, the balance of their contribution being stated as some form of surplus. The shares themselves may be given no par value, which means theoretically that they represent no particular amount of money contribution, but rather a certain fractional interest in the total equity. In many cases nowadays, a low par value is arbitrarily assigned to the shares, largely to reduce incorporation fees and transfer taxes.

These various practices may be illustrated by assuming that the stockholders of a company pay in $10,000,000 in exchange for 100,000 shares of capital stock. Under former procedure the shares would undoubtedly have been given a par value of $100, and the balance sheet would have shown the following:

> Capital, 100,000 shares, par $100 $10,000,000

More recently, the shares might have been given no par value, and the entry would have read:

> Capital, 100,000 shares, no par. Stated value $10,000,000

Or the incorporators might have decided arbitrarily to state the capital at a smaller figure, say, one-half of the amount paid in. In that case, the entries would read:

> Capital, 100,000 shares, no par. Stated value $5,000,000
> Capital surplus (or paid-in surplus)   5,000,000

The most "modern" arrangement would be to give the shares an arbitrarily low par, say, $5. Hence we would see the following peculiar balance sheet setup:

> Capital, 100,000 shares, par $5 $ 500,000
> Capital surplus   9,500,000

In present-day balance sheets, therefore, the division between capital and surplus may be quite meaningless. For most purposes of analysis it is best to take the capital and the various kinds of surplus items together, giving a simple figure for the total equity of the stockholders.

We shall point out later that from the standpoint of the common stockholder an existing preferred-stock issue is more likely to represent a liability of the enterprise than a part of the capital and surplus and also that modern methods of stating that liability on the balance sheet often grossly understate the effective burden involved.

5

Current Assets

Current assets are those which are immediately convertible into cash or which, in the due course of business, tend to be converted into cash within a reasonably short time. (The limit usually set is a year.) Sometimes they are called liquid or quick or floating assets. Current assets group themselves into three broad classes: (1) cash and its equivalents; (2) receivables, i.e., money which is due to the company for goods or services sold; or (3) inventories held for sale or for the purpose of conversion into goods or services to be sold. In the operation of the business these assets change gradually into cash. For example, in a later balance sheet the present inventory would have become cash and receivables, while the present receivables would probably have become cash. Current assets are usually shown on the balance sheet in the relative order of their liquidity.

To give the picture in somewhat more detail, the following list of current asset items is shown, grouped for convenience into the three classes mentioned above.

1. Cash and equivalents:
   Cash on hand or in bank
   Special deposits
   Government & municipal securities
   Other marketable securities
2. Receivables:
   Accounts receivable
   Notes receivable

      Interest receivable
      Due from agents
   3. Inventories:
      Finished goods ("salable")
      Work in progress ("convertible")
      Materials and supplies ("consumable")

Certain kinds of receivables may be relatively noncurrent—e.g., amounts due from officers and employees, including stock subscriptions. If such accounts are not due to be received by the company within a year, they are usually shown separately from the current assets.

On the other hand, it is customary to include the full amount of installment accounts receivable in the current assets, even though a good part may be due later than one year from the date of the balance sheet. Similarly, the entire merchandise inventory is included in the current assets, although some of the items may be slow moving. (However, a footnote to the balance sheet usually indicates what part of the receivables are due after one year.)

6

Current Liabilities

Corresponding to the current assets are the current liabilities. For the most part these are the debts contracted by the company in the ordinary course of operating the business, and presumably are payable within a year, at most. In addition, all other kinds of debts maturing within a year's time are included among the current liabilities.

Those most generally encountered may be described as follows:

Accounts payable are the various amounts of money owed by the corporation to those with whom it does business.

Income taxes accrued are the unpaid portion of income (and sometimes excess profits) taxes due on various dates in the ensuing year.

Money borrowed from banks or others for a short term will be listed as *bank loans* or *notes payable*.

In addition, that portion of originally long-term debt which must now be paid within a year will properly appear among the current liabilities.

Other current liabilities include primarily accrued expenses such as salaries and wages. (These are stated separately by U.S. Steel.) Also dividends payable, customer advances, and the like.

7

Working Capital

In studying what is called the "current position" of an enterprise, we never consider the current assets by themselves, but only in relation to the current liabilities. The current position involves two important factors: (1) the excess of current assets over current liabilities, known as the net current assets or the working capital, and (2) the ratio of current assets to current liabilities, known as the current ratio.

The working capital is found by subtracting the current liabilities from the current assets. Working capital is a consideration of major importance in determining the financial strength of an industrial enterprise, and it deserves attention also in the analysis of public utility and railroad securities, especially where there are large short-term borrowings.

In the working capital is found the measure of the company's ability to carry on its normal business comfortably and without financial stringency, to expand its operations without the need of new financing, and to meet emergencies and losses without disaster. The investment in plant account (or fixed assets) is of little aid in meeting these demands. Shortage of working capital, at its very least, results in slow payment of bills with attendant poor credit rating, in curtailment of operations and rejection of desirable business, and in a general inability to "turn around" and make progress. Its more serious consequence is insolvency and the bankruptcy court.

The proper amount of working capital will vary with the volume of sales and the type of business. The chief point of comparison is

TABLE 3
NET SALES PER DOLLAR OF WORKING CAPITAL
U.S. MANUFACTURING CORPORATIONS
December 31, 1973
(millions of dollars)

	Net Sales	Working Capital	Net Sales per Dollar of Working Capital
All manufacturing corporations	$1,017,163	$190,050	$ 5.35
Bakery products	7,747	564	13.73
Dairy products	17,383	1,669	10.41
Food & kindred	143,551	16,226	8.85
Lumber & wood products	27,387	3,754	7.29
Motor vehicles & equipment	88,879	12,721	6.99
Petroleum refining	96,479	14,925	6.46
Apparel & finished products	31,974	5,170	6.18
Primary iron & steel	40,815	6,986	5.84
Paper & allied products	26,503	4,717	5.62
Fabricated metal products	55,082	10,184	5.41
Stone, clay & glass products	26,072	4,816	5.41
Printing & publishing	31,839	5,950	5.35
Aircraft & parts	29,494	5,625	5.24
Furniture & fixtures	11,599	2,236	5.19
Rubber & miscellaneous plastics	26,410	5,289	4.99
Textile mill products	29,199	6,040	4.82
Electrical machinery	92,053	19,670	4.68
Alcoholic beverages	11,884	2,661	4.46
Tobacco manufactures	12,205	2,770	4.41
Leather & leather products	6,795	1,551	4.38
Basic chemicals	39,612	9,178	4.31
Primary nonferrous metals	25,469	5,933	4.29
Miscellaneous manufacturing	11,747	2,755	4.26
Metal working machinery	7,451	1,800	4.14
Machinery	88,419	23,752	3.72
Instruments & related products	21,504	6,848	3.14
Drugs	15,188	5,070	2.99
All Mfg. Corps.— December 31, 1963	$412.6 bil.	$96.5 bil.	$4.28

The figures for All Manufacturing Corporations for the year ended December 31, 1963, are added at the bottom of each table for comparative purposes.

SOURCE: Federal Trade Commission and Securities and Exchange Commission.

the amount of working capital per dollar of sales. Food companies, enjoying a rapid turnover of inventory, will have high sales per dollar of working capital.

The ratio "sales per dollar of working capital" is used in comparative analysis. The financial position is more readily determined by the current ratio and quick ratio described in Chapter 8.

The working capital is also studied in relation to fixed assets and to capitalization, especially the funded debt and preferred stock. A good industrial bond or preferred stock is expected, in most cases, to be entirely covered in amount by the net current assets. The working capital available for each share of common stock is an interesting figure in common stock analysis especially when this figure (after deducting all prior securities) exceeds the market price of the common. The growth or decline of the working capital position over a period of years is also worthy of the investor's attention.

In the field of railroads and public utilities, the working capital item is not scrutinized as carefully as in the case of industrials. The nature of these service enterprises is such as to require relatively little investment in receivables or inventory (supplies). It has been customary to provide for expansion by means of new financing rather than out of surplus cash. A prosperous utility may at times permit its current liabilities to exceed its current assets, replenishing the working capital position a little later as part of its financing program.

The careful investor, however, will prefer utility and railroad companies that consistently show a comfortable working capital situation.

The working capital of a corporation is *increased* by (1) the amount of the net income, (2) the cash which flows from the annual provision for depreciation and depletion, (3) the funds raised through the sale of securities, (4) deferred taxes, and (5) sometimes by the sale of noncurrent assets.

Working capital is *decreased* by the amount expended for new plant and equipment (or other noncurrent assets), for debt retirement and the like, and dividends paid on preferred and common stocks.

United States Steel Corporation in its Summary of Financial Operations for 1973 gave the following detailed changes in working capital:

TABLE 4
UNITED STATES STEEL CORPORATION
SUMMARY OF 1973 FINANCIAL OPERATIONS

Working capital, December 31, 1972	$556,438,537
Additions to working capital	
Income	$325,757,697
Depreciation & depletion	357,958,348
Deferred taxes	2,164,239
Proceeds from sale of plant	20,460,828
Increase in long-term debt	113,220,003
Total additions	819,561,115
Deductions from working capital	
Plant expenditures	435,501,420
Increase in investments	51,706,073
Dividends on common stock	92,085,154
Decrease in long-term debt	208,473,331
Miscellaneous deductions	5,359,840
Total deductions	793,125,818
Increase in working capital	$ 26,435,297
Working capital, December 31, 1973	$582,873,834

8

Current Ratio

One of the most frequently used figures in analyzing balance sheets is the ratio between current assets and current liabilities. This is usually called the current ratio, and is obtained by dividing the total current assets by the total current liabilities. For example, if the current assets are $500,000 and the current liabilities are $100,000, the current ratio is 5 to 1, or simply 5. When a company is in a sound position, the current assets will exceed the current liabilities by a good margin, indicating that the company should have no difficulty in taking care of its current debts as they mature.

What constitutes a satisfactory current ratio varies to some extent with the line of business. In general, the more liquid the current assets, the less the margin needed above current liabilities. Railroads and public utilities have not generally been required to show a large current ratio, chiefly because they have small inventories and their receivables are promptly collectible. In industrial companies a current ratio of 2 to 1 has been considered a sort of standard minimum.

Many companies reduce their tax liabilities on the balance sheet by subtracting therefrom U.S. tax anticipation notes acquired for that purpose. Without this deduction, the current ratios would in many cases fall below 2 to 1. Where there are U.S. government securities on the asset side and accrued taxes on the liability side, the analyst would be justified in offsetting one against the other to arrive at an adjusted current ratio.

The current ratio should be generally analyzed further by separating out the inventory. It is customary to require that the cash items and the receivables together exceed all the current liabilities. This is the so-called acid test. (There is a tendency now to apply the term "quick assets" to these current assets exclusive of inventory.) If the inventory is of a readily salable kind, and particu-

TABLE 5

CURRENT AND QUICK RATIOS OF U.S. MANUFACTURING CORPORATIONS
December 31, 1973

	Current Assets (millions)	Current Liabilities (millions)	Current Ratio	Quick Ratio
All manufacturing corps.	$386,021	$195,971	1.97x	1.10x
Leather & leather products	2,531	980	2.58	1.26
Drugs	8,327	3,257	2.56	1.64
Instruments & related products	11,565	4,716	2.45	1.51
Paper & allied products	8,849	3,732	2.37	1.54
Primary nonferrous metals	10,326	4,393	2.35	1.38
Furniture & fixtures	3,919	1,683	2.33	1.22
Textile mill products	10,724	4,684	2.29	1.20
Alcoholic beverages	4,751	2,090	2.27	1.07
Basic chemicals	16,776	7,598	2.20	1.36
Stone clay & glass products	8,877	4,061	2.18	1.37
Printing & publishing	11,088	5,138	2.16	1.64
Machinery	44,386	20,634	2.15	1.15
Tobacco manufactures	5,233	2,463	2.12	0.52
Metal working machinery	3,458	1,657	2.09	1.09
Rubber & miscellaneous plastics	10,527	5,238	2.01	1.07
Apparel & finished products	10,318	5,148	2.00	1.05
Fabricated metal products	20,456	10,272	1.99	1.05
Miscellaneous manufacturing	5,547	2,792	1.99	1.10
Primary iron & steel	14,482	7,496	1.93	1.18
Lumber & wood products	7,827	4,073	1.92	1.06
Dairy products	3,584	1,915	1.87	1.02
Food & kindred	35,321	19,095	1.85	0.93
Electrical machinery	43,249	23,579	1.83	0.93
Motor vehicles & equipment	28,816	16,095	1.79	0.87
Petroleum refining	36,205	21,280	1.70	1.30
Bakery products	1,477	913	1.62	0.99
Aircraft & parts	16,428	10,803	1.52	0.45
All Mfg. Corps.— December 31, 1963	$162.7 bil.	$66.2 bil.	2.5x	1.4x

SOURCE: Federal Trade Commission and Securities and Exchange Commission.

larly if the nature of the business makes it very large at one season and quite small at another, the failure of a company to meet this latter "quick asset test" may not be of great importance.

In every such case, however, the situation must be looked into with some care to make sure that the company is really in a comfortable current position.

The ratio of current assets excluding inventory to current liabilities may be called the "quick ratio." Table 5 gives the current and the quick ratios at the end of 1973 for various industries.

Note in Table 5 that the current ratio of the tobacco companies is above average at 2.12 times but that the quick ratio of 0.52 times is less than half the average. The reason is that these enterprises must hold raw-tobacco inventories for a multi-year curing period; hence their inventories represent an unusually large part of their current assets. (See Tables 7 and 8.) With the petroleum refining companies the situation seems to be the reverse.

9

Cash

No useful separation can be made between cash proper and the other "cash assets" or "cash equivalents," consisting of certificates of deposit, call loans, marketable securities, etc. For practical purposes the various kinds of cash assets may be considered interchangeable. In theory, a company should not keep any more cash assets on hand than are required for the transaction of its usual business plus a reasonable margin for emergency requirements. In addition, companies with bank borrowings are usually required to maintain a proportionate cash deposit—say 20%—with the lending bank. These amounts are called "compensating balances." But many companies tend to hold more cash than the business seems to need. Much of this surplus cash is held in the form of marketable securities. The current return on these investments is usually small. They may yield substantial profits (or losses) due to market changes, but such operations are not properly part of the ordinary commercial or manufacturing business.

A shortage of cash is ordinarily taken care of by bank borrowings. In the usual case, therefore, a weak financial position is likely to be shown more through large bank loans than through insufficient cash on hand. During recessionary stages in the economy it is particularly important to watch the cash account from year to year. Companies frequently build up their cash account even during periods of operating losses by liquidating a large part of their other assets, especially inventories and receivables. Other concerns show a serious loss of cash or—what amounts to the same thing—a substantial increase in bank loans. In such periods the way in

19

which the losses reflect themselves in the balance sheet may be more important than the losses themselves.

Where the cash holdings are exceptionally large in relation to the market price of the securities, this factor usually deserves favorable investment attention. In such a case the stock may be worth more than the earning record indicates, because a good part of the value is represented by cash holdings which may contribute comparatively little to the income account. Eventually the stockholders are likely to get the benefit of these cash assets, either through their distribution or their more productive use in the business.

10

Receivables

The relative amount of receivables varies widely with the type of industry and the trade practices in paying up accounts. Also, in certain lines of business, receivables are likely to vary with the conditions of bank credit; that is, when bank loans are hard to get the amount of receivables increases as the company extends more than the usual amount of credit to its customers.

As in the case of inventories, receivables should be studied in relation to the annual sales and in relation to changes shown over a period of years. Any sudden increase in receivables as a percentage of sales may indicate that an unduly liberal credit policy is being followed in an effort to sustain the volume.

The FTC-SEC 1973 report shows that the manufacturing companies used in its sample had receivables at year-end 1973 of $139.3 billion against annual sales of $1,017.2 billion. Reducing the annual volume to net daily sales and dividing this amount into the receivables indicates that the accounts were being liquidated in about fifty days.

The accounts receivable require the most careful scrutiny in the case of companies selling goods on a long-term payment basis. This group includes department stores, credit chains, and mail-order houses. Farm implements, trucks, and office equipment are also sold on long-term credits. Much of this installment business is carried on through finance companies which advance funds against the notes or guarantee of the seller. In most cases the finance company exacts a repurchase agreement from the manufacturer. In these instances neither the receivable nor the debt appears directly

21

on the balance sheet of the manufacturer but is referred to in a footnote. In analyzing the balance sheet such discounted receivables should be given full consideration as the equivalent of both assets and liabilities.

TABLE 6

LIQUIDATION PERIOD FOR RECEIVABLES
U.S. MANUFACTURING CORPORATIONS
December 31, 1973
(dollars in millions)

	Sales	Receivables	Liquidating Period
All manufacturing corporations	$1,017,163	$139,342	50 days
Motor vehicles & equipment	88,879	6,810	28
Tobacco manufactures	12,205	926	28
Bakery products	7,747	620	29
Dairy products	17,383	1,381	29
Food & kindred	143,551	12,194	31
Lumber & wood products	27,387	2,497	33
Paper & allied products	26,503	2,993	41
Primary iron & steel	40,815	4,878	44
Aircraft & parts	29,494	3,621	45
Apparel & finished products	31,974	3,956	45
Alcoholic beverages	11,884	1,486	46
Furniture & fixtures	11,599	1,545	49
Leather & leather products	6,795	922	49
Stone, clay & glass products	26,072	3,664	51
Fabricated metal products	55,082	7,935	52
Primary nonferrous metals	25,469	3,663	52
Textile mill products	29,199	4,363	54
Printing & publishing	31,839	5,217	60
Rubber & misc. plastics	26,410	4,375	60
Basic chemicals	39,612	6,430	61
Petroleum refining	96,497	16,394	62
Metal working machinery	7,451	1,269	62
Electrical machinery	92,053	16,459	65
Machinery	88,419	16,048	66
Instruments & related products	21,504	4,023	68
Drugs	15,188	2,876	69
Miscellaneous manufacturing	11,747	2,372	74
All Mfg. Corps.— December 31, 1963	$412.6 bil.	$51.5 bil.	45 days

SOURCE: Federal Trade Commission and Securities and Exchange Commission.

11

Inventories

Inventories comprise goods held for sale or in process of manufacture and materials and supplies used up in operating the business. For manufacturing companies the figure is generally broken down into categories of raw materials, work in process, and finished goods. It is ordinarily the largest of the current items and at year-end 1973 accounted for 43 % of the current assets of U.S. manufacturing corporations (Table 7).

The chief criterion of inventory soundness is the turnover, defined as the annual sales divided by the year-end inventory.[1] The standards on this point vary widely for different industries. The range of variation among industries and a norm for individual lines is supplied in Table 7. The comparison of inventory turnover among companies within an industry will in many cases reveal an important competitive advantage which marks the leading companies in the group. But this fact in itself is not conclusive unless all the companies being compared are using the same basis for valuing their inventory.

The two important ways of calculating inventory values are known as "first-in, first-out" (FIFO) and "last-in, first-out" (LIFO). The difference between them turns on how the cost of the items on hand is calculated. This basic difference is generally illustrated by a company's coal pile. If the coal bought is piled on top and the coal used is taken from the bottom, we have a typical case

---

[1] The true turnover is found by dividing the inventory into the cost of sales, but it is customary to use the total sales instead of the cost of sales. This accepted turnover is thus always larger than the true figure.

of first-in, first-out. The old coal is used up first, and the stock that remains would naturally be valued on the basis of the most recent

TABLE 7

INVENTORY TO CURRENT ASSETS

U.S. MANUFACTURING CORPORATIONS

December 31, 1973

(dollars in millions)

	Current Assets	Inventory	Inventory to Assets
All manufacturing corporations	$386,021	$170,875	44 %
Printing & publishing	11,088	2,665	24
Petroleum refining	36,205	8,551	24
Paper & allied products	8,849	3,089	35
Drugs	8,327	2,987	36
Stone, clay & glass products	8,877	3,329	37
Bakery products	1,477	567	38
Basic chemicals	16,776	6,454	38
Instruments & related products	11,565	4,453	38
Primary iron & steel	14,482	5,625	39
Primary nonferrous metals	10,326	4,385	42
Miscellaneous manufacturing	5,547	2,472	44
Dairy products	3,584	1,628	45
Lumber & wood products	7,827	3,509	45
Machinery	44,386	20,119	45
Rubber & miscellaneous plastics	10,527	4,904	46
Apparel & finished products	10,318	4,907	47
Fabricated metal products	20,456	9,610	47
Furniture & fixtures	3,919	1,872	48
Textile mill products	10,724	5,118	48
Metal working machinery	3,458	1,654	48
Electrical machinery	43,249	21,186	49
Food & kindred	35,321	17,524	50
Motor vehicles & equipment	28,816	14,762	51
Leather & leather products	2,531	1,296	51
Alcoholic beverages	4,751	2,517	53
Aircraft & parts	16,428	11,559	70
Tobacco manufactures	5,233	4,000	76
All Mfg. Corps.— December 31, 1963	$162.7 bil.	$70.5 bil.	43 %

SOURCE: Federal Trade Commission and Securities and Exchange Commission.

purchases. But if we assume the coal used is taken off the top we would have the typical last-in-, first-out situation. The coal on

TABLE 8

INVENTORY TURNOVER

U.S. MANUFACTURING CORPORATIONS

December 31, 1973

(dollars in millions)

	Net Sales	Inventory	Turnover Rate[a]
All manufacturing corporations	$1,017,163	$170,875	5.9
Bakery products	7,747	567	13.7
Printing & publishing	31,839	2,665	11.9
Petroleum refining	96,497	8,551	11.3
Dairy products	17,383	1,628	10.7
Paper & allied products	26,503	3,089	8.6
Food & kindred	143,551	17,524	8.2
Lumber & wood products	27,387	3,509	7.8
Stone, clay & glass products	26,072	3,329	7.8
Primary iron & steel	40,815	5,625	7.2
Apparel & finished products	31,974	4,907	6.5
Furniture & fixtures	11,599	1,872	6.2
Basic chemicals	39,612	6,454	6.1
Motor vehicles & equipment	88,879	14,762	6.0
Primary nonferrous metals	25,469	4,385	5.8
Fabricated metal products	55,082	9,610	5.7
Textile mill products	29,199	5,118	5.7
Rubber & miscellaneous plastics	26,410	4,904	5.4
Leather & leather products	6,795	1,296	5.2
Drugs	15,188	2,987	5.1
Instruments & related products	21,504	4,453	4.8
Miscellaneous manufacturing	11,747	2,472	4.7
Alcoholic beverages	11,884	2,517	4.7
Metal working machinery	7,451	1,654	4.5
Machinery	88,419	20,119	4.4
Electrical machinery	92,053	21,186	4.3
Tobacco manufactures	12,205	4,000	3.0
Aircraft & parts	29,494	11,559	2.5
All Mfg. Corps.—December 31, 1963	$412.6 bil.	$70.5 bil.	5.8

[a] Annual sales divided by year-end inventory.

SOURCE: Federal Trade Commission and Securities and Exchange Commission.

hand at the inventory date would represent some old or original purchase, and it could be valued at an unchanging price from year to year.

The LIFO method was introduced about 1941 in order to avoid marking up inventories to reflect the war-induced rise in the price level. It is widely felt that such gains in inventory values are illusory and are likely to be followed by corresponding losses when the price pendulum swings downward. An additional object of importance is to avoid paying income tax on such questionable "profits."

However, the majority of companies have adhered to the older, and in some respects more natural, FIFO method. This has introduced a complication into statement analysis, particularly in the comparison of two companies using different bases of inventory valuation. As long as prices advance, the FIFO company will tend to show better earnings than the LIFO company, and its stated asset value will be correspondingly higher. These advantages are reversed when the price level turns downward, for then the FIFO company begins to show inventory losses which the other concern is spared.

The current issue of *Accounting Trends and Techniques*, which covers the year 1972, reports that of the 600 companies it reviews, 150 were using LIFO for valuing all or part of their inventory.

The difference made in the reported results by the choice of LIFO as against FIFO accounting becomes more or less important as the rate of inflation increases or subsides. For the year 1973 about one-sixth of corporate profits before taxes were ascribable to inflationary gains in inventory values. Just how an item of this type should be treated poses a difficult problem for the analyst.

12

Current Liabilities (Notes Payable)

The total amount of current liabilities is of interest only in relation to the current assets. You have already seen the importance of the current ratio (total current assets to total current liabilities) and the desirability of having the quick assets (exclusive of inventory) exceed the current liabilities.

The most important individual item among the current liabilities is notes payable. This generally represents bank loans, but it may also apply to certain trade accounts or to borrowings from affiliated companies or from individuals. The fact that a company has borrowed from the banks is not in itself a sign of weakness. Seasonal borrowings, which are entirely paid off after the close of the active sales period, are considered desirable from the viewpoints both of the company and the banks. But more or less permanent bank loans, even though they may be well covered by current assets, are likely to be an indication that the company is in need of long-term capital in the form of bonds or stock.

Where the balance sheet shows notes payable, the situation must always be studied with greater care than is otherwise called for. If the notes payable are substantially exceeded by the cash holdings, they can ordinarily be dismissed as relatively unimportant. But if the borrowings are larger than the cash and receivables combined, it is clear that the company is relying heavily on the banks. Unless the inventory is of unusually liquid character, such a situation may justify misgivings. In such a case the bank loans should be studied over a period of years to see whether they have been growing faster than sales and profits. If they have, it is a definite sign of weakness.

13

Property Account (Fixed Assets)

The property account of a corporation includes land, buildings, equipment of all kinds, and office furnishings. These are often referred to as the "fixed assets," although many are quite movable, such as locomotives, floating equipment, small tools, etc. The proportion of the total assets taken up by the property account varies widely with different types of businesses. The property investment of a railroad is very large, while the property account of a finance company is likely to be an insignificant part of the total assets.

In nearly all companies the property account is carried at a conservative figure. The usual basis is actual cost less depreciation. In many cases plants were marked down in the depression of the 1930s to figures well below their cost. Important amounts of new plant were written off in full by the accelerated amortization permitted under the tax laws during World War II and were similarly written down under emergency legislation renewed during the Korean conflict. In 1954, depreciation was liberalized, and the write-off of new plant equipment was permitted at double the former rates. In the 1960s new tax rulings shortened the so-called useful life of many categories of fixed assets, again increasing the allowed depreciation. As a result, property accounts now stand on most corporate books at unrealistically low values.

Because of the frequent wide differences between book value and reproduction value, stockholders should be supplied with more information regarding the present value of the property account than is contained in the ledger figures. We suggest that if the insured value of the plant and property were given as a footnote to the balance sheet, a much more informative picture of the plant account would be available to those who really own the assets.

Years ago it was not uncommon to find arbitrarily high values placed on the fixed assets—values which bore little relation to their actual cost or subsequent fair value. For example, the property account of the United States Steel Corporation was originally marked up or inflated by an amount in excess of $600 million. This gave the common stock a fictitious book value, and the epithet "watered stock" was commonly applied to inflated capitalization of this kind. (Subsequently the "water" was taken out of the property account of United States Steel by various kinds of special charges against earnings and surplus.) In contrast to the watered accounts of the past, present-day balance sheets carry plant accounts at levels that might be called dehydrated.

During the past fifty years investors have come to pay less and less attention to the asset values shown by a company and to place increasing weight upon its earnings record and earnings prospects. This change in attitude was due in part to the frequent unreliability of the property-account figure in the past, but it had separate justification in the fact that, for the typical going business, value does reside in earning power much more than in assets.

We think the pendulum has swung too far in the direction of ignoring balance sheet values. The property account should neither be accepted at face amount nor overlooked entirely. It deserves reasonable consideration in appraising the company's securities.

14

Depreciation and Depletion in the Balance Sheet

All fixed assets are subject to a gradual loss of value through age and use. The allowance made for this loss in value is known variously as depreciation, obsolescence, depletion, and amortization.

Depreciation applies to the ordinary wearing out of buildings and equipment. *Obsolescence* refers to an extra-rapid loss of value due to technological and similar changes. *Depletion* applies to the gradual removal of mineral and timber resources by turning them into products for sale. It is charged by mining enterprises, oil and gas companies, sulphur and lumber producers, and many others. *Amortization* is a general term applied to all deductions of the depreciation type, but it also connotes special kinds of charge-offs, e.g., "accelerated amortization" of defense facilities.

Allowances for depreciation, etc., appear both as a charge against earnings in the income account and as a deduction from the original value of the fixed assets in the balance sheet. In industrial companies the accumulated depreciation is subtracted directly from the fixed-asset account on the left side of the balance sheet. In utility and railroad accounting it often appears as an offsetting entry on the right or liability side.

The original cost of the property, without allowance for depreciation, is called the gross value. The figure obtained after deducting accrued depreciation is called the net value. When property is retired or sold, its gross value is deducted from the property account, and the depreciation accrued against it is taken out of the accumulated depreciation. This explains why the accumulated depreciation on the balance sheet may not increase in a given period by the full amount charged as amortization against earnings.

The more important aspects of the annual allowances for depreciation and depletion will be discussed in our section on the income account.

Let us point out that the overall figures for balance sheet depreciation for All Manufacturing Corporations have not changed much in the last decade: It was 51 % of the gross plant in 1963 and 47 % in 1973. That for U.S. Steel was 59 % in 1963 and 55 % in 1973.

15

Noncurrent Investments
(Intermediate Assets)

Many companies have important investments in other enterprises, in the form of securities or advances. Some of these investments are of the same sort as are made by the ordinary buyer of securities, namely, readily marketable bonds and stocks which are held for income or market profit and which may be sold at any time. Such investments are usually listed among the current assets as "marketable securities."

Other investments, however, are made for purposes related to the company's business. They consist of stocks or bonds of affiliated or subsidiary companies, or loans or advances made to them. A consolidated balance sheet eliminates the securities held in *wholly-owned* (and now in *majority-owned*) subsidiary companies, including instead the actual assets and liabilities of the subsidiaries as if they were part of the parent company. Where the subsidiary is not wholly-owned, the minority interest appears as a quasi liability, or offset, on the right side of the balance sheet. There is now a tendency to apply this treatment to enterprises in which the parent company has working control even where its equity ownership is less than half. This is called the *equity method* of accounting.

In other cases the interest in partly-owned subsidiary enterprises will appear in the balance sheet under the heading of noncurrent investments and advances, or the like.

These items are usually shown on the balance sheet at cost, though they frequently are reduced by reserves set up against them, and in fewer cases are increased to allow for accumulated profits. It is difficult to estimate the true value of these investments. Where it appears from the balance sheet that these items are likely to be of importance, a special effort should be made to obtain additional information regarding them.

Many industrial companies have realty, leasing, and finance subsidiaries that are not in the parent's balance sheet on a consolidated basis, even though wholly-owned or nearly so. Each appears only as an asset at its net equity value, and thus their liabilities— often very substantial and mainly current—are not stated at all, except sometimes in explanatory notes. The purpose and result of this accounting method is to make the company's working-capital and debt position appear better than it actually is. Some of these investments have required guarantees of obligations of the affiliates, and these also do not appear as parent-company liabilities. Such items, when large, may require careful consideration by security analysts.

Some investments stand midway between ordinary marketable securities and the typical nonmarketable permanent commitment in a related company. This intermediate type is illustrated by the large investment of Union Pacific in the securities of other railroads. Such holdings will appear among the intermediate assets rather than the current assets, since the companies regard them as permanent investments; but for some purposes (e.g., calculating the quick assets per share of stock) it is permissible to regard them as the equivalent of readily marketable securities.

16

Intangible Assets

Intangible assets, as the name applies, are those which cannot be touched or measured in physical terms. The most common intangibles were formerly good will, trademarks, patents, and leaseholds. Somewhat distinct from the concept of good will proper is the concept of going-concern value, the special profit-making character that attaches to a well-established and successful business. Trademarks and brands constitute a rather definite type of good will, and they are generally referred to as part of the good-will picture. An investor should recognize a very strong distinction between good will as it appears—or, more generally, fails to appear—on the balance sheet, and good will as it is measured and reflected by the market price of the company's securities or by the analyst's valuation of the enterprise.

The treatment of good will on the balance sheet varies among different companies. The most usual practice nowadays is either not to mention this asset at all or to carry it at the nominal figure of $1. In some cases good will has actually been acquired at a definite cost in the original purchase of the business from its former owners, and it is then feasible to show the good will at cost in the same manner as other assets.

When one company acquires another, the purchase price frequently exceeds the book value of the assets of the acquired company. This excess is generally classified as purchased good will and is set up in the balance sheet as an asset to be written off against income over a period of years, generally ten to twelve. We regard this practice as completely illogical.

34

The modern tendency is not to ascribe any value to good will on the balance sheet. Many companies which started with a substantial good-will item have written this down to $1 by making corresponding reductions in their surplus or even their capital accounts.

This writing down of good will does not mean that it is actually worth less than before, but only that the management has decided to be more conservative in its accounting policy. This point illustrates one of many contradictions in corporate accounting. In most cases the writing off of good will takes place after the company's position has improved. But this means that the good will is, in fact, considerably more valuable than it was at the beginning.

Patents constitute a somewhat more definite form of asset than good will. But it is extremely difficult to decide what is the true or fair value of a patent at any given time, especially since we rarely know to what extent the company's earning power is dependent on any patent that it controls. The value at which the patents are carried on the balance sheet seldom offers any useful clue to their true worth.

The "leasehold" item is supposed to represent the cost or money value of long-term leases held at advantageous rentals, i.e., rentals at lower rates than similar space could be leased. But in a period of declining real estate values, long-term leaseholds are just as likely to prove to be liabilities as assets, and the investor should be chary of accepting any valuation ascribed to that item.

In general, it may be said that little if any weight should be given to the figures at which intangible assets appear on the balance sheet. Such intangibles may have a very large value indeed, but it is the income account and not the balance sheet that offers the clue to this value. In other words, it is the earning power of these intangibles, rather than their balance-sheet valuations, that really counts to an extent perhaps greater than is true of other elements in the book value.

17

Prepaid Expense and Deferred Charges

In most balance sheets prepaid expense and deferred charges appear together at the bottom of the list of assets. Because the amount of money they involve is small, they are frequently excluded in computing asset values, such as the book value of stock or the tangible-asset protection for bonds.

Prepaid expense items differ somewhat from deferred charges in that the former are tangible assets, and they may even properly be considered current assets. They represent amounts paid to others for services to be rendered in the future and thus will be incorporated in future operating expenses in the same way as raw materials and other assets. If these services are terminated in advance of completion, the items would have some residual or surrender value to the corporation.

Fire insurance premiums, for example, are frequently paid in advance for periods of five years. During the first year, one-fifth of the expense is charged to operations, with the remaining four-fifths listed in the balance sheet as prepaid expense. In each succeeding year, the asset is then reduced by one-fifth the original amount until the entire item is written off against operations. Prepaid rentals on property are handled in the same way. The American Institute of Certified Public Accountants has suggested that prepaid-expense items (chargeable to earnings within a year) be included in the current assets—as the equivalent of accounts receivable—and they are now beginning to be treated in this fashion.

Deferred charges, in contrast to prepaid expense, represent amounts paid for which no specific service will be received in the future but which are nonetheless considered properly chargeable to future operations. The expense of moving a plant might logically be amortized over a period of five years. Bond discount is usually written off over the life of the bond issue. Whatever the item may be, each year's expense is charged with a proper proportionate share, and the balance is carried in the balance sheet as a deferred charge.

18

Reserves

It is useful to divide reserves into three classes:

1. Liability reserves, which represent a more or less definite obligation.
2. Valuation reserves, which are offsets against the stated value of some asset.
3. Surplus or "voluntary" reserves, which merely set aside part of the reinvested earnings.

Reserves of the first class are set up for taxes, for accident claims and other pending litigation, for refunds to customers and similar obligations, and for certain future operating charges, such as relining blast furnaces. These are for the most part semicurrent liabilities, but in many cases they are separated from the current liabilities in the balance sheet and appear in an intermediate position.

The most important valuation reserves are those for depreciation and depletion, which we have already discussed. Another offsetting reserve is that for losses on receivables, or "reserve for bad accounts." This is deducted directly from the accounts or notes receivable, and frequently the amount taken off is not stated.

In former days a third important offset reserve was that for decline in inventories, but this is rarely encountered now. In dealing with such a reserve it is essential to know whether it reflects a decline that has already taken place or merely one that may be expected. If the former is true, the inventory must be considered as definitely reduced by the amount of the reserve. But if the reserve is set up to take care of a possible *future* decline in value it must be viewed rather as a reserve for contingencies, which is in reality part of the retained earnings.

The same point may be made with respect to reserves against marketable securities and other investments. Here, too, it is important to know if they reflect a past and actual, or merely a possible, decline in value.

An item of increasing importance among deferred charges is the amount paid out as "past-service cost of pensions." This is the starting-up cost of a pension fund and in some cases is substantial. The U.S. Treasury Department has ruled that under tax regulations such amounts may be written off against future income over a period of not less than ten years. Sound and informative financial statements should, in the first year of this pension expense, charge off one-tenth (or less) immediately and show nine-tenths (or more) of the past-service cost as a deferred charge to be deducted from income in subsequent installments. This method maintains reported income in line with income tax provisions—an important check point for analysts.

On the other hand, many companies have liabilities for accrued or vested pension costs which are not provided for in the balance sheet. Where the amount is important it requires consideration by analysts.

Contingency reserves and other similar reserves tend to make corporate statements confusing, because they obscure the time and effect of various kinds of losses. If in one year a company sets up a reserve for future decline in inventory value, it seems proper to take this reserve out of surplus rather than charge it to earnings, since the loss has not actually been realized. But if in the next year a decline in inventory takes place, it seems proper again to charge this loss against the reserve set up for that contingency. It follows that the loss, although actually incurred, is not charged against income in any year, and to that extent, the earnings for the period have been overstated.

To avoid being deceived by these devices the analyst must examine both the income statement and the reinvested earnings over several years and make due allowance for any amount charged to surplus (retained earnings) or reserves which really represents business losses during the period.

Now and then the balance sheet contains items such as "reserve for plant improvement," "reserve for working capital," "reserve for preferred stock retirement," etc. Reserves of this sort represent neither a debt nor a definite deduction from any asset. They are clearly part of the surplus account. The purpose in setting them up is usually to indicate that these funds are not available for distribution to the stockholders. If this is so, such reserves may be considered "appropriated surplus."

Since 1948, there has been a perceptible trend toward simplifying and rationalizing financial statements. Among the steps taken is a strong drive in the direction of eliminating reserves of various kinds from the balance sheet. The thinking on the subject may be summarized as follows: (1) Valuation reserves should be deducted directly—as "allowances"—from the affected asset; (2) reserves which represent real or probable liabilities should be classified as current liabilities or as reserves for specified contingencies; (3) those of an indefinite nature should be returned to earned surplus.

However, significant fluctuations in foreign-exchange rates have brought alternating profits and losses to companies with substantial foreign interests. There is now a new tendency to transfer such profits made in one year to a reserve for foreign exchange fluctuations, or the like, to absorb corresponding losses in future years.

19

Book Value or Equity

The book value (or "asset protection") of a security is in most cases a rather artificial value. It is assumed that if the company were to liquidate, it would receive in cash the value at which its various tangible assets are carried on the books. Then the amounts applicable to the various securities in their due order would be their book value, or in the case of bonds and preferred stocks, their "asset protection." (The word "equity" is frequently used instead of book value in this sense, but it is generally applied only to common stocks and to speculative senior securities.)

As a matter of fact, if the typical company were actually liquidated, the realized value of the assets would probably be less than their book value as shown on the balance sheet. An appreciable loss is likely to be realized on the sale of the inventory, and a substantial shrinkage is usually suffered in the value of the fixed assets. In most cases the adverse conditions that would lead to a decision to liquidate the business would also make it impossible to obtain anywhere near cost for the plant and the machinery. In recent years there have been exceptions to this rule, because the higher price level has created so wide a margin between reproduction cost and book value that sometimes the total assets can be liquidated at an actual profit.

The book value really measures, therefore, not what the stockholders could get out of their business (its liquidating value), but rather what they have put into the business, including undistributed earnings. The book value is of some importance in analysis because there may be some relationship between the amount invested in a business and its future average earnings or its realized value. It is true that in many individual cases we find companies with small asset values earning large profits, while others with large asset values earn little or nothing. Yet in these cases some attention must be given to the book value situation. For there is always a possibility that large earnings on the invested capital may attract competition and thus prove temporary; also that large assets, not now earning profits, may later be made more productive, or they may be merged, sold as a whole, or liquidated piecemeal for well above the depressed market level of the stock.

We think that stock market developments in recent years have restored a substantial degree of practical value to the book value figure of many enterprises. More than half of the New York Stock Exchange issues seem to have sold both above and below book value during the 1968–1974 period. Hence for many companies now the book value (or net asset value) may be taken as a useful

TABLE 9

	1968–1974		1973 Book Value		1968–1974		1973 Book Value
	High	Low			High	Low	
Allied Chemical	54	16	33	Int'l. Harvester	40	17	46
Alcoa	56	24	41	Int'l. Nickel	48	21	16
Amer. Brands	50	28	36	Int'l. Paper	57	26	27
Amer. Can	58	22	37	Johns-Manville	46	14	28
Amer. Tel & Tel	58	40	49	Owens-Illinois	81	27	47
Anaconda	66	11	47	Procter &			
Bethlehem Steel	37	19	52	Gamble	120	40	21
Chrysler	73	9	50	Sears, Roebuck	123	44	32
Du Pont	203	92	69	Std. Oil of Calif.	45	19	34
Eastman Kodak	152	58	19	Texaco Inc.	45	20	29
Esmark	45	20	38	Union Carbide	52	29	35
Exxon	103	46	59	United Aircraft	83	21	47
General Electric	76	30	19	U.S. Steel	49	25	70
General Foods	47	16	18	Westinghouse	55	8	22
General Motors	91	32	44	Woolworth	56	10	30
Goodyear Tire	35	12	23				

point of departure for determining buy and sell points for their shares.

The relationship between the price range and the 1973 book value of the thirty issues in the Dow-Jones Industrial Average during 1968–1974 is given in Table 9. Six of the stocks sold consistently above book value while three sold consistently below that figure. During the seven-year period, nineteen have sold above or below the most recent book value. Two—General Foods and International Paper—would be considered marginal in this context.

20

Calculating Book Value

The book value per share of a common stock is found by adding up all the assets (excluding intangibles), subtracting all liabilities and stock issues ahead of the common, and then dividing by the number of shares. In most cases the book values may be computed readily from the conventional published balance sheet.

As an alternative, it is sufficient to add together the common stock at par or stated value, the various surplus items, and the voluntary reserves, and to subtract any arbitrary items for intangibles. This will give the total common stock equity, which is then divided by the number of shares.

Adjustment may be made, if desirable, to correct the stated liability for preferred stock. The proper calculation of this liability often presents a problem. The simplest rule to follow is to value stocks with preference claims at the highest of their par value, call price, or market price. Where there are preferred dividend arrears, these should be deducted as well in arriving at the book value for common.

Allegheny Ludlum Industries Inc. $3 cumulative preferred stock, Par $1, convertible into common share for share, was callable at 64 in 1974 and later at 60. On December 31, 1973, 2,017,000 shares were outstanding. At mid-year 1974 the common stock was priced in the market at 28 and the preferred stock sold at 38.

This issue appears on the balance sheet as a liability of $1 per share on $2,017,000. The true liability is of course much higher. On a minimum callable and liquidation-value basis it would be $60 a share or $121 million. The effect of this markup would be to reduce the book value of the common from the balance-sheet figure of $56.70 per share to a corrected $31.77 per share.

Under 1974 conditions the actual burden of the $3 preferred might well be considered at less than $60 per share, but it is always best to be conservative in these matters. On the other hand, when the common sold at 79 in 1967 the various calculations would then have assumed conversion of the preferred into common.

21

Tangible Asset Protection
for Bonds and Preferred Stocks

The Alcoa Balance Sheet is used to illustrate asset value computations for senior securities.

ALUMINUM COMPANY OF AMERICA
CONDENSED BALANCE SHEET
December 31, 1973
(thousands of dollars)

Working capital	$ 597,132	Debt	$ 884,415
Net plant	1,530,167	Preferred stock	
Other assets	385,233	(659,909 shares)	65,991
		Equity (33,074,535 shares)	1,562,126
Net working assets	$2,512,532	Invested capital	$2,512,532

The tangible asset position is the sum of the bonds at par value, the preferred stock and the common stock, and surplus. Intangibles on the asset side, if any, would be deducted from the total. The balance is then divided by the number of bonds outstanding.

(000 omitted)

Bonds	$ 884,415
Preferred stock	65,991
Common stock	33,075
Additional capital	66,402
Retained earnings	1,462,649
Total tangible assets for bonds	$2,512,532
Tangible assets per $100 bond	284
Tangible assets for preferred stock	1,628,117
Tangible assets per $100 of pfd.	2,467

46

It is customary to calculate the book value or tangible assets per share of preferred stock in a similar fashion as for the common. But this will give misleading results when there are substantial amounts of bonds outstanding. In fact it may make the preferred stock appear better protected than the bonds. For example, by this method the net tangible assets for Alcoa bonds are given as $284 for each $100 of debt while the assets for the preferred stock are given as $2,467 per $100 share—over eight times that for the bonds.

The better method would be to compute the overall asset coverage for the debt and preferred stock combined in the same way as is done in calculating earnings coverage on bond interest and preferred dividends. The bonds and preferred stock at stated value total $950.4 million. This amount divided into the available assets of $2.512 billion indicates combined asset coverage equal to 264 % for the bonds and preferred stock taken together.

The asset coverage of the bonds and preferred stock of Alcoa is comfortable and is in line with the ratios for senior securities of other industrial companies.

22

Other Items in Computing Book Value

In calculating the book value of a security, the various forms of surplus are all treated as one. For example, a company might show capital surplus, appropriated surplus, premium on stock sold, and profit and loss or earned surplus. These would all be added together and regarded as surplus.

In the chapter on reserves, it was mentioned that certain kinds of reserves are really a part of the surplus. These include reserves for contingencies (unless they relate to a definite and reasonably probable payment or loss of value), general reserve, reserves for dividends, reserves for preferred stock retirement, reserves for improvements, reserves for working capital, etc. Reserves for insurance may also properly be considered in the same class, but reserves for pensions are usually a true liability and should not be included as part of the surplus.

These reserves equivalent to surplus (sometimes called "voluntary reserves") should be added in with the surplus in figuring the book value. In finding the net book value all the intangibles should be deducted. Such deferred charges as organization expense and unamortized bond discount should also be excluded.

23

Liquidating Value
and Net Current Asset Value

Liquidating value differs from book value in that it is supposed to make allowance for loss of value in liquidation. It is obviously impractical to talk of the liquidating value of a railroad or the ordinary public utility. On the other hand, the liquidating value of a bank, insurance company, or typical investment trust (or investment holding company) may be calculated with a fair to high degree of accuracy, and if the figure is well above the market price this fact may be of real importance.

In the case of industrial enterprises, the liquidating value may or may not be a useful concept, depending on the nature of the assets and the capitalization setup. It is particularly interesting when the current assets make up a relatively large part of the total assets and the liabilities ahead of the common are relatively small. This is true because the current assets usually suffer a much smaller loss in liquidation than do the fixed assets. In some cases of liquidation it happens that the fixed assets realize only about enough to make up the shrinkage in the current assets.

Hence the "net current asset value" of an industrial common stock is likely to constitute a rough measure of its liquidating value. It is found by taking the net current assets (or "working capital") alone and deducting therefrom the full claims of all senior securities. When a stock is selling at much less than its net current asset value, this fact is always of interest, although it is by no means conclusive proof that the issue is undervalued.

24

Earning Power

For many decades in the past book value has played only a minor part in the analysis of a common stock. (The chief exceptions have been financial companies—banks, insurance companies, and particularly investment funds.) In the great majority of instances the attractiveness or the success of an equity investment will be found to depend on the earning power behind it. Even if, as we have previously suggested (pages 42–43), the book value may now furnish a good starting point for investment decisions for many common stocks, the book figure will have validity only to the extent that it is supported by the earning power of the shares.

The term "earning power" should be used to mean the earnings that may reasonably be expected over a period of time in the future. Since the future is largely unpredictable, we are usually compelled to take either the current or past earnings as a guide and to use these figures as a base in making a reasonable estimate of future earnings.

If there have been reasonably normal business fluctuations for a period of years, the average of the earnings over the period will afford a better index of earning power than the current figure alone, but conservative allowance may be made for the growth factor up to the current date. The average is the best figure to use if the purpose is to determine whether a bond or a preferred stock constitutes a safe investment.

In the next few chapters the elements of an earning statement will be discussed.

25

A Typical Industrial Income Account

UNION CARBIDE CORPORATION
CONSOLIDATED STATEMENT OF INCOME AND RETAINED EARNINGS
Year Ended December 31, 1973
(millions of dollars)

Net sales	$3,938.8
Deductions:	
Production costs and distribution expense	2,592.0
Research and development	76.8
Selling, administrative, and other expense	426.2
Depreciation and depletion	245.2
	3,340.2
Income from operations	598.6
Other income (net)	10.3
Interest on long- and short-term debt	60.6
Income before provision for income taxes	548.3
Provision for income taxes:	
Current	219.5
Deferred	24.4
Total	243.9
Pre-tax income	304.4
Less	
Minority holders share of income	24.5
	279.9
Plus	
Share of income of companies carried at equity	11.0
Net income	290.9
Retained earnings January 1	1,618.0
	1,908.9
Dividends declared	126.1
Retained earnings December 31	$1,782.8

51

26

A Typical Railroad Income Account

All railroad reports are made to the Interstate Commerce Commission on a uniform basis in accordance with rules adopted by that body. But in certain instances they require restatement by the security analyst to make them more informative and even more accurate. We present herewith the 1973 income account of Union Pacific Railroad Co., first on the basis filed with the I.C.C. and then in the form we recommend for analysis.

UNION PACIFIC R.R. CO.
Year Ended December 31, 1973
(thousands of dollars)

Operating revenues	$870,723
Operating expenses	644,928
Revenues over expenses	225,995
Railway tax accruals	86,924
Railway operating income	139,071
Equipment rents (cr)	14,076
Joint facility rents (dr)	1,805
Other income	5,881
Gross income	157,223
Miscellaneous deductions	4,945
Balance for charges	152,278
Fixed charges	26,555
Net income	125,723

The key items of expense and their relation to operating revenues are listed below.

	(thousands of dollars)	percent of revenues
Maintenance of way	$113,492	13.0 %
Maintenance of equipment	155,834	17.9
Transportation	307,090	35.0
All other	68,512	7.9
Total	$644,928	73.8 %

Joint facility rents represent amounts paid (dr) or received (cr) for the use of terminal facilities or trackage with another carrier. Equipment rents refer to payments made and payments received to and from other railroads (and private owners) for the use of rolling stock—freight and passenger cars and locomotives. Both types of rentals are combined with other income to form the "intermediate items."

UNION PACIFIC R.R. CO.
SUGGESTED PRESENTATION OF A RAILROAD INCOME STATEMENT
Year Ended December 31, 1973
(thousands of dollars)

Operating revenues	$870,823
Primary expenses	444,682
Balance	426,241
Maintenance	269,326
Operating income	156,915
Intermediate items (cr)	18,152
Balance	175,067
Miscellaneous deductions	4,945
Balance for charges	170,122
Fixed charges	26,555
Pre-tax income	143,567
Federal income tax	17,844
Net income	$125,723

27

A Public Utility Income Account

OKLAHOMA GAS AND ELECTRIC COMPANY
STATEMENT OF INCOME
Year Ended December 31, 1973
(thousands of dollars)

Electric Revenues	$198,731
Operating expenses:	
Operation	74,442
Maintenance	9,313
Depreciation	21,158
Federal income tax	16,980
Deferred income tax (net)	6,049
Investment tax credits (net)	2,153
Other taxes	19,787
Total operating expenses	149,882
Operating income	48,849
Other income and deductions:	
Interest income	988
Allowance for funds used during construction	2,427
Miscellaneous	(770)
Other income (net)	2,645
Interest charges:	
Interest on long-term debt	14,593
Other	644
Total interest charges	15,237
Net income	$ 36,257

STATEMENT OF RETAINED EARNINGS
BALANCE
January 1, 1973

Add	
	$71,124
Net income	36,257
Total	107,381

Deduct

Preferred dividends	2,518
Common dividends	23,801
Other debits	436
Total	26,755
Balance December 31, 1973	$80,626

The Oklahoma Gas and Electric Company's statement of income for 1973 is typical of those public utility companies whose state commission permits the use of normalized accounting. Both federal and deferred income taxes are listed in the income statement. The deferred portion is carried over to the balance sheet and added to the item Deferred Federal Income Taxes. Deferred taxes result from the use of accelerated depreciation in the tax return. The net effect is to reduce the income taxes payable during the early service life of the property but to increase taxes payable in later years. As the tax allowed charge for depreciation declines the company will draw on the reserve to pay the increased taxes.

The investment tax credit is an amount equal to 4 % of annual plant expenditures which may be used to reduce federal income taxes. The company may use each year's credit against the year's income taxes or it may spread the credit over the life of the asset which created the credit. At mid-year 1974, Congress was considering a request to increase the credit to 7 %—the amount allowed industrial companies.

Other state public utility commissions compel companies under their jurisdiction to follow less conservative methods. The tax deferrals, for example, are not transferred to a reserve but are treated as earnings. The investment tax credit is applied each year in full to reduce income taxes (and increase reported earnings).

An item of unusual interest in the economy of the mid-1970s is the Allowance for Funds used during Construction. This item arises from the fact that during the time a utility plant is under construction the capital involved is earning no return although the annual cost has to be paid for and is a part of the cost of building the facility. In practice, an amount equal to the interest cost of the money involved is added to the income statement. This is a paper credit; no cash is received. The importance of A.F.D.C. is a by-product of current events. In 1963, the A.F.D.C. of a group of forty-seven utility companies came to 4.8 % of the balance for common. In 1973, the fifty companies which are closely followed by Argus Research Corporation reported A.F.D.C. equal to 32 % of balance for common. This latter figure reflects the high cost of larger amounts of plant and the wide increase in interest rates. In some cases, earnings less the A.F.D.C. credit fall below the annual dividend. One or two companies have received permission to treat plant under construction as part of the working rate base and are allowed the regular rate of return thereon. This may or may not represent a permanent solution.

Beginning in 1973, in footnotes to their financial statements, many utility companies published a reconciliation of the effective federal income tax rate paid by the company with the statutory rate of 48 %. Oklahoma Gas and Electric whose reported rate was 41 % attributed the tax savings as follows: Accelerated depreciation 1.7 %; A.F.D.C. (which is not taxable as income) 1.9 %; amortization of investment tax credit 1.4 %; and miscellaneous items which aggregated 2 %—a total of 7 %.

28

Calculating Earnings

In studying a bond issue, the most important figure is the number of times the total interest charges (and equivalent) are earned. Charges of the same nature as bond interest (such as "other interest," adjusted rentals, amortization of bond discount) should be included therewith, and the number of times these "fixed charges" are covered should be computed. (In dealing with the bonds of holding companies it is usually necessary to consider the subsidiaries' preferred dividends as fixed charges, for these may have to be paid before there is any income available for the parent company's bonds.)

The coverage of interest or fixed charges is calculated, of course, by dividing these charges into the earnings available for them. The method of calculating earnings coverage is complicated by the question whether earnings before or after taxes should be used. Under tax laws interest payments on debt are deducted before arriving at the amount of profits subject to income tax. Increases or decreases in the rate of federal taxation would not therefore influence the ability of the company to meet the fixed charges on its bonds. Hence, earnings available for interest charges should properly be shown before deducting income taxes, and the coverage should be calculated from that figure.

In many corporate reports to stockholders, including nearly all railroads and public utilities, it is customary to reverse this order and to show the amount of earnings available for interest charges after deduction of income taxes. But the income tax figure is either shown or easily determinable, and the proper adjustment can readily be made by adding back the tax figure before computing coverage.

In the case of a senior bond issue it may be useful, on occasion, to compute the interest coverage without counting the charges on junior bonds. This is a supplementary figure, however, and must always be studied in conjunction with the total interest on all the issues outstanding (the "overall" coverage); for, ordinarily, no bond issue can be strong if the enterprise as a whole is weak. It is never correct to calculate the coverage on a junior issue alone, after deducting from income the requirements of the senior issue. This may give very misleading results, and in the case of a small junior issue may indicate that it is safer than the senior issues, which is manifestly absurd.

Where there is a preferred stock issue not preceded by bonds, the earnings available for it may be shown either as dollars earned per share, or the number of times the dividends were covered. (The latter method has more to recommend it.) To find the preferred dividend coverage, simply divide the net income available for dividends by the dollar amount of the preferred dividend requirements.

However, if there are bonds outstanding, the preferred dividend coverage should be calculated only in conjunction with the fixed charges. In other words, you must calculate how many times the total of fixed charges plus preferred dividends was earned. It is common practice in these cases to calculate the coverage of preferred dividends separately, but that method is incorrect in the case of issues bought for investment and may give rise to seriously misleading results.

Consideration should be given the fact that preferred dividends (in contrast to bond interest) are paid after taxes and that changes in the corporate income tax rate may affect the ability of some companies to pay dividends. Under the present tax structure (1974) corporations are required to earn approximately $2 before taxes to meet each dollar of preferred dividend requirements.

In the interest of simplifying the coverage test for preferred stocks preceded by bonds, we recommend that the following formula be used:

1. To the fixed charges add an amount equal to twice the preferred dividend requirements. (The doubling of the preferred dividend is an arithmetic offset to compensate for the tax disadvantage of preferred stocks. The addition of such a tax component gives the same basic coverage for a preferred stock as the coverage *before taxes* of a corresponding bond.

2. The total of fixed charges plus the preferred dividends doubled is then divided into the amount available for fixed charges.

Common stock earnings are always shown as so much a share. They are computed after deducting preferred dividends at the full annual rate to which the issue is entitled (including the participating feature, if any), whether paid or not. (Back dividends on a preferred stock are not deducted from current earnings in figuring the amount available for the common, but the existence of such accumulated dividends must, of course, be taken into account.)

29

The Safety of Fixed Charges and Preferred Dividends

In analyzing an investment-grade bond, the coverage of the fixed charges (before income tax) is the main criterion. In the case of a high-grade preferred stock, the comparable test is the coverage of the sum of twice the preferred stock dividends and the fixed charges.

Minimum required coverages should be set high enough to provide reasonable assurance of safety and should reflect variations in the inherent stability of the several major types of enterprises—public utilities, railroads, and industrials.

The following tests are recommended for investment-grade bonds:

1. Average earnings, before income taxes, for a period covering the most recent seven years should equal the lesser of the following multiples of fixed charges or the following percentage of debt principal:

Type of Enterprise	Coverage of Charges	Seven-year Average (earned on principal of debt)
Public utility	4 times	28 %
Railroad	5 times	35 %
Industrial	7 times	50 %

2. Alternatively, the earnings before income taxes of the *poorest year* in the seven-year period should equal the lesser of the following multiples of fixed charges or the following percentage of debt principal:

Type of Enterprise	Charges Earned	Poorest-year Test (earned on principal of debt)
Public utility	3 times	20 %
Railroad	4 times	28 %
Industrial	5 times	35 %

60

For investment-grade preferred stocks the same minimum figures as above are required to be shown by the ratio of earnings before income taxes to the sum of the fixed charges plus twice preferred stock dividends.

(The coverage figures suggested in our table are more stringent than those generally accepted. We recommend them, nevertheless, because experience suggests that investors in fixed-rate securities have suffered losses in the past which can be traced to acceptance of inadequate earnings protection.)

In an investment study of the income account, attention is given the following additional factors among others:

1. The major indication of the prosperity of a business is found in the rate of return shown on invested capital. The figure most in use relates to the earnings percentage on common-stock equity, i.e., the ratio of common-stock earnings to its book value. Another measure in use is the rate of earnings on total capital, including long-term debt and preferred stock.

2. The operating ratio, a figure obtained by dividing the operating expenses by the total revenue or sales. In the analysis of industrial companies it is customary to consider the profit margin, which is the complement of the operating ratio. Both figures provide a measure of the operating efficiency of the company and also of its ability to absorb reductions in volume or in selling price.

3. The ratio of fixed charges (or fixed charges and preferred dividends) to gross revenues.

4. The maintenance and depreciation charges.

5. The nature and amount of charges to surplus not included in the income account.

In studying these figures comparisons should be made between various companies in the same field and for the same company for successive years.

These ratios and others are illustrated and discussed in Part III of this book.

30

Maintenance, Depreciation, and Similar Factors in the Income Account

A thoroughgoing analysis of an income account would take into consideration a number of factors which we have not space to discuss. But the subject of maintenance and depreciation must be given a fair amount of attention even in an elementary text such as this. By making excessive or insufficient allowances for these items the net earnings may readily be understated or overstated. It is important to remember that depreciation charges differ from other operating expenses in that they are not actually laid out in cash, but are book entries deducted from the profits, on one hand, and from the property account, on the other. However, they *do* apply to expenditures which were actually made in cash in prior years and which must be charged off against income as the assets wear out or otherwise lose their value. Hence depreciation and similar charges are by no means imaginary or unnecessary deductions; failure to provide for them would produce entirely misleading results.

The tax law permits several different basic methods of calculating amortization, and different percentage rates may be admissible within the same method. In addition, companies frequently take greater or less depreciation in their published reports than is used in their tax returns.

Maintenance expense ordinarily represents a direct cash outlay similar to any other expense. In the case of industrial companies it is taken for granted that current maintenance is kept up to date, and the figure is not separately examined. But in railroading, where maintenance outlays absorb about a third of operating revenues, there is room for considerable variance in policy between one road and another and from year to year in the same road. Thus the "maintenance ratio" receives considerable emphasis in railroad analysis. This figure includes depreciation. In the case of public utilities, the maintenance charge or ratio is usually studied in conjunction with the separately stated provision for depreciation.

SOME HIGHLIGHTS ON DEPRECIATION POLICY

The most common depreciation method is the "straight-line" basis, which writes off the cost of the property (less expected salvage) in equal amounts each year over the estimated life of the asset.

Example: If machinery is installed at a cost of $100,000, with an expected life of eight years and a probable final salvage value of $10,000, the annual depreciation charge on a straight-line basis would be ⅛ × $90,000 ($100,000 less $10,000). This gives $11,250 as the annual depreciation charge. Typical straight-line depreciation rates for important kinds of property include: buildings, 2–5 %; machinery, 7–20 %; furniture and fixtures, 10–15 %; automobiles and trucks, 20–25 %; etc.

More liberal depreciation charges in the early years are permitted by the "declining balance" method. The initial annual rate may be as high as one and a half times the straight-line rate when applied to property constructed prior to 1954, and twice the straight-line rate against property completed after 1953. Using our previous example and applying it to new machinery purchased after 1953, the law would now allow charging off 25 % of the undepreciated balance in each year. This would give successive annual deductions of $22,500, $16,875, $12,657, etc. At a given time the company will exercise its right under the tax law to change over to the straight-line basis. Otherwise it could not write off the full cost of the asset (less salvage) by the end of its useful life.

Somewhat similar results would be obtained by a third permissive method known as the "sum of the digits." Under this method the digits represent the remaining property life to the beginning of each year. Thus the digits for property with a five-year life are 5, 4, 3, 2, 1, the sum of these numbers being 15. Depreciation expense for the first year is five-fifteenths of the cost of the property; for the second year four-fifteenths of the cost; and for the third year, three fifteenths of the cost; etc.

Furthermore, many facilities installed during World War II and since the Korean War received certificates of necessity under which most of their total cost could be amortized by sixty equal monthly charges, i.e., in five years. This was known as "accelerated amortization." Many of the railroads made equipment purchases subject to certificates of necessity. However, by an inexcusable ruling of the Interstate Commerce Commission on this matter, the carriers are required to overstate their true earnings. They may deduct from income only the "normal" depreciation on their facilities, and at the same time they must include in profits the taxes saved by applying the higher, accelerated rates. This applies also to the faster depreciation permitted by the tax laws since 1954.

At times in the past certain companies charged off more depreciation than was allowed by the tax regulations. Conversely, it was frequent practice to understate the required depreciation, especially through the use by public utilities of the so-called "retirement reserve method." Both of these practices have now become quite rare.

We should mention that many corporation executives insist that depreciation charges should be large enough to *replace* the property worn out and thus reflect increases in the price level (inflation). However, both the accounting profession as a whole and the tax laws insist that depreciation allowances should return only the original dollar cost of each asset. It would be a desirable addition to company reports to include therein a statement of the gross and net value of the fixed asset at current replacement costs and the annual depreciation based on such value.

The relationship between gross value of the property account and annual depreciation in 1973 for various manufacturing indus-

TABLE 10

DEPRECIATION RATES

U.S. MANUFACTURING CORPORATIONS

December 31, 1973

(dollars in millions)

	Gross Value of Property, Plant, and Equipment	Annual Provision for Depreciation & Depletion	Col. 1 ÷ Col. 2
All manufacturing corporations	$529,091	$32,894	6.2 %
Machinery	43,267	3,965	9.2
Motor vehicles & equipment	35,637	3,217	9.0
Apparel & finished products	3,788	323	8.5
Instruments & related products	12,146	1,017	8.4
Miscellaneous manufacturing	3,050	252	8.3
Leather & leather products	1,213	92	7.5
Lumber & wood products	12,174	882	7.2
Electrical machinery	33,333	2,399	7.2
Furniture & fixtures	2,910	193	6.6
Printing & publishing	12,551	834	6.6
Fabricated metal products	20,211	1,317	6.5
Textile mill products	13,024	849	6.5
Aircraft & parts	10,357	653	6.3
Rubber & miscellaneous plastics	13,448	843	6.3
Metal working machinery	3,311	209	6.3
Basic chemicals	37,846	2,282	6.0
Dairy products	4,186	243	5.8
Food & kindred	40,100	2,344	5.8
Stone, clay & glass products	19,005	1,058	5.6
Paper & allied products	19,998	1,012	5.1
Petroleum refining	109,467	5,625	5.1
Alcoholic beverages	5,135	260	5.1
Tobacco manufactures	3,979	202	5.1
Bakery products	3,420	168	4.9
Drugs	6,819	337	4.9
Primary nonferrous metals	21,252	912	4.3
Primary iron & steel	38,211	1,524	4.0
All Mfg. Corps.— December 31, 1963	$232,777 mil.	$13,545 mil.	5.8 %

SOURCE: Federal Trade Commission and Securities and Exchange Commission.

tries is shown in Table 10. Note that in most categories the figures vary between 4.2 % and 9.7 % and average 6.2 %. There has been some increase in the overall depreciation rate since 1963.

DEPLETION

Depletion, like depreciation, is a rather complicated affair. For tax purposes a company may ordinarily choose the most liberal of three possible methods, as applied to each separate depletable property, as follows:

In ordinary *cost depletion*, the company deducts that percentage of the cost of the property which the minerals extracted bear to the total estimated content. In *percentage depletion*, the company may deduct either a specified percentage of the gross income from the property (e.g., 22½ % for oil, 15–23 % for metal mines), or 50 % of the net income, whichever is lower. In *discovery depletion,* the original cost of the property is marked up to a higher value established by the discoveries of mineral content after the purchase was made; and such larger value is amortized in lieu of cost. Many metal-mining companies do not deduct their tax-allowed depletion from the income reported to stockholders.

DEVELOPMENT EXPENSE

Many oil and mining companies reduce their income taxes sharply by taking advantage of the privilege of charging against profits all development costs incurred each year. Moreover, most of them do not make this immediate charge-off in their published statements but instead spread the cost over a number of years in the future. Furthermore, the majority of the oil companies do not follow what we would consider the standard and proper accounting practices: namely, to deduct from the earnings a provision for future taxes equivalent to the taxes currently saved. The inference is that the reported earnings of many oil companies are overstated in somewhat the same way as those of the railroads, as previously discussed.

In thorough analysis, these methods of accounting for various kinds of amortization and development expense must be carefully examined.

CASH FLOW

Cash flow may be defined as the net income of a business plus the depreciation and other amortization previously deducted—i.e., the net income before deduction of such charges. Much emphasis has been placed on this figure by security analysts in recent years. It is a useful figure in a detailed comparison of different companies in the same industry and sometimes for comparing the results for the same company over a span of years. However, the cash flow is often presented on a per share basis, with the implication that it represents the "true earnings" of the business. Such an inference would be completely wrong.

As indicated at the outset of this chapter the depreciation, etc., actually sustained in any period is as much a charge against earnings as any other expense. The only difference is that the cash expenditures now being charged off were made in a previous year, when the property was acquired, instead of in the current year. In the case of dry holes charged off by oil companies, and tooling costs written off over a short period by manufacturing companies, the actual cash expenditures involved may be current or quite recent.

In our view the average investor would do well to ignore the cash-flow figure, as it is more likely to mislead than to enlighten him. Security analysts should study these figures mainly to determine whether the amortization charges need revision as being either too high or too low from the comparative standpoint.

31

The Income Tax Factor in the Income Account

The rate of federal income tax on corporations in 1974 and for a number of years past has been 48 %. There are also state income taxes in forty-six states varying from 1 % to 12 %. (These are treated as expense items before computing income subject to federal tax.) However, the actual rate of tax paid by many companies is less than 48 % of their reported income before tax. There are three legitimate ways in which a corporation may reduce its tax burden below the standard percentage:

1. It may have types of income subject to a lesser tax rate. Examples:

   a. Interest on state and municipal obligations is exempt from all federal income tax.

   b. Most dividends received from other U.S. companies are taxable on only 15 % thereof, i.e., at 7.2 % of the amount received.

   c. The income earned abroad by international corporations may be subject to lower tax rates than their domestic earnings.

Also the actual tax paid is reduced in many cases by the permitted carry-forward or offset of past net losses; but present accounting rules require that such benefits be shown separately in the income statements as the equivalent of nonrecurring items.

2. The company may take allowable deductions on its income tax returns which are larger than those shown in its report to stockholders. Examples:

a. Accelerated depreciation on income tax returns versus lower, straight-line rates in its annual reports.

b. Research and development expense, especially for technological concerns and oil companies. (These may be charged off as incurred in the tax returns but capitalized and written off gradually in the reports to stockholders.)

c. Percentage depletion allowed to oil and other mineral producers.

3. The income tax liability may be reduced by an investment tax credit amounting, in 1974, to 7 % of expenditures for new plant and equipment.

Congressional moves have been underway to reduce certain of the tax advantages enjoyed by corporations. In cases where the reported tax is well under the 48 % rate, the analyst must study the reasons for the difference and decide to what degree, if any, it may call into question the validity or the permanence of the reported earnings before and after taxes.

32

The Trend of Earnings

A consistent change in some important factor in the income account over a period of time is known as a trend. The most important trends for our purpose are those of interest-and-preferred-dividends coverage and of earnings available for the common stock; but these trends result in turn from favorable or unfavorable trends in the gross business, operating ratio, and fixed charges.

Obviously it is desirable that a company show a favorable trend in net earnings and particularly in earnings per share. (The companies themselves seem to place major emphasis on their annual growth in sales, but if such growth is achieved by a sacrifice of profitability it can harm rather than help the stockholders.) Senior securities of a company revealing a definitely unfavorable trend should not be bought for ordinary investment, even though the coverage may still be adequate, unless you are convinced that the trend will correct itself shortly. On the other hand, there is danger of attaching undue importance to a favorable trend, for this too may prove deceptive. In the case of investment issues it is well to require in every case that the *average* earnings show a satisfactory coverage for interest and preferred dividends.

In selecting common stocks it is proper to assign more weight to the indicated trend than in the purchase of senior issues, for a common stock can advance substantially in price if the trend continues. However, before purchasing a common stock because of its favorable trend it is well to ask two questions: (1) How certain am I that this favorable trend will continue? (2) How large a price am I paying in advance for the expected continuance of the trend?

33

Common Stock Prices and Values

Broadly speaking, the price of common stocks is governed by the prospective earnings and dividends. In the typical case the earnings will determine the dividends. The prospective earnings are, of course, a matter of estimate or forecast; and the action of the stock market on this point is usually controlled by the indicated trend. The trend is usually gauged in turn from the past record and current data, although at times the expectation of some quite new development will play a determining part.

The price of common stocks will depend, therefore, not so much on past or current earnings in themselves as upon what the security-buying public thinks the future earnings will be. (There are also important influences of a general or technical nature affecting stock prices—such as credit and political and psychological conditions—which may not be closely related to any estimate of future earnings; but such influences will either eventually reflect themselves in the earnings or else prove to be quite temporary.)

In the ordinary case the price of a common stock is the resultant of the many estimates of what the earnings are going to be in the next six months, in the next year, or farther in the future. Some of these estimates may be entirely incorrect and some may be exceedingly accurate; but the buying and selling by the many people who make these various estimates is what mainly determines the present price of a stock.

The accepted idea that a common stock should sell at a certain ratio to its current earnings must be considered more the result of practical necessity than of logic. The market takes the trend or future prospects into account by varying this ratio for companies with different characteristics. The chief factor has long been the expected future growth rate which in turn has been largely determined by the actual growth rate of per share earnings in the past. In Table 11, we show the price-earnings ratio (or multipliers) for the thirty Dow-Jones Industrial stocks in 1963 and at the close of

TABLE 11
DOW-JONES INDUSTRIAL AVERAGE

	Average Earnings 1961–63	Price Dec. 31, 1963	P/E Ratio	Average Earnings 1971–73	Price Dec. 31, 1973	P/E Ratio
Allied Chem.	$ 2.44	54¾	22.4x	$ 2.57	49	19.1x
Alcoa	1.49	45⅞	30.9	2.60	48½	18.6
Amn. Brands	2.51	28½	11.3	4.59	32¼	7.0
Amn. Can	2.68	43⅝	16.3	3.06	26¼	8.6
Amn. Tel. & Tel.	2.87	69⅝	24.2	4.43	50⅛	11.3
Anaconda	2.11	23⅜	11.1	1.72	26⅛	15.2
Beth. Steel	2.15	30¾	14.3	3.62	33	9.1
Chrysler	2.07	41⅝	20.1	3.58	15⅝	4.4
Du Pont	9.51	200	21.0	9.23	159	17.2
Eastman Kodak	0.85	29	34.1	3.34	116	34.7
Esmark	1.27	21¾	17.1	2.92	24⅞	8.5
Exxon	4.04	76	18.8	8.16	94⅛	11.5
Gen'l. Electric	1.47	43½	29.6	2.91	63	21.6
Gen'l. Foods	1.56	45	28.8	2.29	23¾	10.4
Gen'l. Motors	4.49	78⅝	17.5	7.52	46⅛	6.1
Goodyear Tire	1.09	20⅝	18.9	2.51	15¼	6.1
Int'l. Harvester	1.86	30	16.1	2.89	25¾	9.2
Int'l. Nickel	1.31	27½	21.0	1.92	35¼	18.3
Int'l. Paper	1.52	32⅛	21.1	2.48	52	21.0
Johns-Manville	1.48	24⅜	16.5	2.73	16½	6.0
Owens-Illinois	2.06	42⅞	20.8	4.09	30⅞	7.5
Procter & Gamble	1.32	40	30.3	3.32	92	27.7
Sears, Roebuck	1.57	49	31.2	3.94	80¼	20.4
Std. Oil of Calif.	1.87	28⅜	15.2	3.73	35	9.4
Texaco	1.83	34⅛	18.6	3.78	29⅜	7.8
Union Carbide	2.51	60¼	24.0	3.57	34⅛	9.5
United Aircraft	1.57	28½	18.1	3.03	23¾	7.8
U.S. Steel	2.97	53⅛	17.9	3.92	37⅝	9.6
Westinghouse	0.68	17	25.0	2.05	25⅜	12.4
Woolworth	1.67	24⅝	14.7	2.74	18⅜	6.7
DJIA	$36.52	762.95	20.9x	$69.45	850.86	12.2x

1973 (in both cases based on three-year average earnings). The variation in the multipliers is surprisingly large. However, the appended data on the change in earnings per share between the 1961–1963 and 1971–1973 periods show that the 1963 multipliers proved to be good indicators, on the whole, of the comparative growth to be realized in the next decade.

When neither boom nor recession nor a pronounced bullish or bearish atmosphere is affecting the market, the judgment of the public on individual issues, as indicated by market prices, is usually fairly good. If the market price of some issue appears out of line with the facts and figures available, it will often be found later that the price is discounting future developments not then apparent on the surface. There is, however, a frequent tendency on the part of the stock market to exaggerate the significance of changes in earnings both in a favorable and unfavorable direction. This is manifest in the market as a whole in periods of both boom and decline, and it is also evidenced in the case of individual companies at other times.

At bottom the ability to buy securities—particularly common stocks—successfully is the ability to look ahead accurately. Looking backward, however carefully, will not suffice and may do more harm than good. Common stock selection is a difficult art, naturally, as it offers large rewards for success. It requires a skillful mental balance between the facts of the past and the possibilities of the future.

34

Conclusion

In the preceding chapters you have seen the various factors to be considered in reading financial statements. By an examination of the statements it is possible to form an opinion as to the present position and potentialities of the company to the extent you assume that past performance will continue into the future. The earning power of the company, the financial position as compared with other companies in the same industry, the trend of earnings, and the ability of the management to meet constantly changing conditions—all these factors have an important bearing on the value of the company's securities. In a number of cases the asset value may be of interest, especially as a basis for determining buy and sell levels for the issue.

However, there are other factors outside the exhibit of the company that have an important influence on the market price and perhaps also on the intrinsic value of its securities. The outlook for the industry, general business conditions, periods of optimism and pessimism in the security markets, artificial market influences, the popular favor of the type of security—these factors cannot be measured in terms of exact ratios and margins of safety. They can be judged only by a general knowledge gained by constant contact with financial and business news.

The investor who buys securities only when their market price looks attractive on the basis of the company's statements and sells them when they look too high on this same basis probably will not make spectacular profits. But, on the other hand, he will probably avoid equally spectacular and more frequent losses. He should have a better-than-average chance of obtaining satisfactory results. And this is the chief objective of intelligent investing.

PART II: Debits and Credits

The understanding of financial statements will be aided by a brief outline of the bookkeeping methods upon which they are based. Bookkeeping, accounting, and financial statements all are based on the two concepts of debit and credit.

An entry which increases an asset account is called a debit, or a charge. Conversely, an entry which decreases a liability account is also called a debit, or a charge.

An entry which increases a liability account is called a credit. Conversely, an entry which decreases an asset account is called a credit.

Since capital and the various forms of surplus are liability accounts, entries increasing these accounts are called credits, and entries decreasing these accounts are called debits.

Business books are kept by what is called the "double-entry system," under which every debit entry is accompanied by a corresponding credit entry. Hence the books are always kept in balance, meaning that the total of asset accounts always equals the total of liability accounts.

The ordinary operations of a business involve various income and expense accounts such as sales, wages paid, etc., which do not appear in the balance sheet. These operating or intermediate accounts are transferred (or "closed out") at the end of the period into surplus or into profit and loss (which is the name given to the surplus account that reflects operating results, dividends, etc.). Since income entries are equivalent to additions to surplus, they appear as credit or liability accounts. Expense entries, which are equivalent to deductions from surplus, appear as debit or asset accounts.

A "trial balance" shows all the various accounts as they appear on the books before the intermediate or operating accounts are closed out into profit and loss. The total of all debit balances must be equal to the total of all credit balances.

The appended simplified case history may be found useful as indicating how the operations of a company are entered on the books, then reflect themselves in the trial balance, and finally are absorbed into the balance sheet. (It is not to be expected that corporate bookkeeping can be adequately treated within the confines of this presentation. Hence, the reader may wish to replace or supplement the following material by reference to some standard textbook on accounting.)

At the beginning of the period Company X showed the following balance sheet:

Cash	$3,000	Capital stock	$5,000
Inventory	4,000	P & L surplus	2,000
	$7,000		$7,000

The ledger (the book in which the accounts are kept), from which the above balance sheet was taken, would appear as follows:

Cash		Inventory		Capital Stock		P & L Surplus	
Dr.	Cr.	Dr.	Cr.	Dr.	Cr.	Dr.	Cr.
$3,000		$4,000			$5,000		$2,000

During the period, it sells on credit for $3,000 goods which cost it $1,800, and incurs various expenses, paid in cash, totaling $500. The original entries, which are made in the journal, are as follows:

Dr. Accounts receivable	$3,000	Cr. Sales	$3,000
Dr. Cost of sales[1]	1,800	Cr. Inventory	1,800
Dr. Expenses	500	Cr. Cash	500

[1] Cost of sales is actually calculated by deducting closing inventory from opening inventory plus purchases. We use the above entry for the sake of simplicity.

At the end of the period the above entries are transferred to the ledger, which will appear as follows:

	Cash		Inventory		Accounts Receivable		Sales	
Dr.	Cr.	Dr.	Cr.	Dr.	Cr.	Dr.	Cr.
$3,000	$ 500	$4,000	$1,800	$3,000			$3,000
	2,500 (to		2,200 (to				
	balance)		balance)				
$3,000	$3,000	$4,000	$4,000				

Cost of Sales	Expenses	Capital Stock	P & L Surplus
$1,800	$500	$5,000	$2,000

From the above the following trial balance would be taken off:

Cash	$ 2,500	Capital stock	$ 5,000
Inventory	2,200	P & L surplus	2,000
Accts. rec.	3,000	Sales	3,000
Cost of sales	1,800		
Expenses	500		
	$10,000		$10,000

The operating accounts are then closed out into profit and loss by the following transfer entries:

Dr. Sales	$3,000	Cr. Profit & loss	$3,000
Dr. Profit & loss	1,800	Cr. Cost of sales	1,800
Dr. Profit & loss	500	Cr. Expenses	500

It will be noted that these result in a net increase of $700 in profit and loss surplus, representing the profit for the period. These entries eliminate the operating accounts. The ledger would now appear as follows:

Cash		Inventory		Accts. Rec.
$3,000	$ 500	$4,000	$1,800	$3,000
	2,500 (to balance)		2,200 (to balance)	
$3,000	$3,000	$4,000	$4,000	
$2,500		$2,200		

	Sales		Cost of Sales		Expenses	
to P & L $3,000	$3,000	$1,800	$1,800 to P & L	$500	$500 to P & L
$3,000	$3,000	$1,800	$1,800	$500	$500

Capital Stock			*P & L Surplus*	
$5,000	(from cost of sales)	$1,800	$2,000	
	(from expenses)	500	3,000	(from sales)
	(to balance)	2,700		
		$5,000	$5,000	
			$2,700	

From the above ledger we would then have the following balance sheet, representing the condition of the company at the close of the period under consideration:

ASSETS		LIABILITIES	
Cash	$2,500		
Inventory	2,200	Capital stock	$5,000
Accts. rec.	3,000	P & L surplus	2,700
	$7,700		$7,700

PART III: *Analyzing a Balance Sheet and Income Account by the Ratio Method*

A number of the ratios used in the analysis of an industrial company's income account and balance sheet are presented here using the financial statements of Bristol-Myers Company for the year ended December 31, 1973. Various items in the statements are numbered to facilitate the explanation of the method of computing ratios.

BRISTOL-MYERS COMPANY
INCOME ACCOUNT
Year Ended December 31, 1973
(thousands of dollars)

(1)	Net sales	$1,362,995
(2)	Cost of sales	1,167,562
	Gross operating income	195,433
(3)	Depreciation	20,175
(4)	Operating income	175,258
	Other income	21,252
(5)	Total income	196,510
(6)	Fixed charges	15,120
	Pre-tax income	181,390
	Income taxes	79,627
(7)	Net income	101,763
(8)	Preferred stock dividends	2,573
(9)	Balance for common	99,190
(10)	Common stock dividends	40,424
	Reinvested earnings	$ 58,766

BRISTOL-MYERS COMPANY
CONSOLIDATED BALANCE SHEET
December 31, 1973
ASSETS
(000)

Current assets:

(11)	Cash and equivalent		$154,442
(12)	Receivables		233,199
(13)	Inventory		219,439
	Other		46,040
(14)	Total current assets		$653,120
(15)	Plant (at cost)	369,082	
(16)	Accumulated depreciation	147,515	
(17)	Net plant		221,567
	Other assets		20,259
	Good will		61,042
	Total		$955,988

LIABILITIES
(000)

Current liabilities:

	Short-term debt	$ 63,150
	Accounts payable	79,339
	Accrued expenses	98,031
	Accrued taxes	53,271
(18)	Total current liabilities	$293,791
	Other liabilities	25,615
(19)	Long-term debt	98,567
(20)	$2 preferred stock (Par $1)	1,287
(21)	Common stock	31,355
(22)	Capital surplus	59,520
(23)	Retained earnings	445,853
	Total	$955,988
(24)	Market price of common per share Dec. 31, 1973	46¼

A. BALANCE SHEET RATIOS

A-3. *Common Stock Ratio*

The sum of the common stock, capital surplus, and retained earnings
divided by the sum of the bonds, preferred stock at redemption
price, common stock, capital surplus, and retained earnings.
Formula: (21) through (23) ÷ (19) through (23).

In this calculation the sum of the items making up the common stock account has been reduced by a charge to the capital account of $63,024,000—the amount required to bring the $2 preferred stock from its $1 par to its redemption price of $50 per share.

$$\$473,704,000 \div \$636,582,000 = 74.4\%$$

A-4. Current Ratio

Current assets divided by current liabilities.
Formula: (14) $\div$ (18)   or
$$\$653,120,000 \div \$293,791,000 = 2.2 \text{ to } 1$$
The standard minimum requirement is 2 to 1.

A-5. Quick Assets Ratio

Current assets less inventory divided by current liabilities.
Formula: (14) $-$ (13) $\div$ (18)   or
$$\$433,681,000 \div \$293,791,000 = 1.5 \text{ to } 1$$
This ratio exceeds the minimum requirement of 1 to 1.

A-6. Book Value of the Common Stock

The sum of common stock, capital surplus, and retained earnings divided by the number of common shares outstanding.
Formula: (21) through (23) $\div$ (21, expressed as shares)
$$\$473,704,000 \div 31,355,000 = \$15.11 \text{ per share}$$
It is customary to exclude intangibles from book value, i.e., they would be deducted from equity before dividing by the number of shares. Bristol-Myers carries a good will item of $61,042,000 representing the excess of the cost over the value of the assets received in an acquisition. The exclusion of this item would reduce book value by $1.95 a share to $13.16.

P-1. Price-Earnings Ratio

Market price of the stock divided by earnings per share. In October of 1974 Bristol-Myers sold at 32, a figure equal to 10.1 times the earnings of 1973 and to 8.6 times the estimate of $3.70 a share for 1974.

B. Income Account and Balance Sheet Ratios

B-1. *Inventory Turnover*

Net sales divided by inventory.

Formula: $(1) \div (13)$ or

$\$1,362,995,000 \div \$219,439,000 = 6.2$ times[1]

Bristol-Myers' inventory turnover runs slightly ahead of the FTC-SEC index of all industries, where the figure for 1973 was 5.9 times.

B-2. *Number of Days Average Account Receivable is Outstanding*

Accounts receivable divided by daily net sales.

Formula: $(12) \div \dfrac{(1)}{365}$ or

$$\$233,199,000 \div \frac{\$1,362,995,000}{365} = 36 \text{ days}$$

This ratio is designed to determine the credit policy of the company. A 36-day liquidation is superior to the FTC-SEC companies where the period is 50 days and a wide improvement over the drug industry total where the collection time is 69 days.

A. Capitalization Ratios

A-1. *Bond Ratio*

Amount of bonds outstanding divided by the sum of bonds, preferred stock, common stock, capital surplus, and retained earnings.

Formula: $(19) \div (19)$ through (23) or

$\$98,567,000 \div \$636,582,000 = 15.5\%$

This is well below the 24.7 % ratio shown by FTC-SEC sampling.

---

[1] The real or physical turnover is found by dividing inventory, which is carried at cost, into cost of sales. Formula: $(2) \div (13)$ or 5.3 times.

A-2. *Preferred Stock Ratio*

Preferred stock divided by the sum of the bonds, preferred stock, common stock, capital surplus, and retained earnings.

Formula: (20) ÷ (19) through (23)

(The preferred stock is carried on the books as a liability at its par value of $1 per share. A realistic figure to use is redemption value of $50 a share for the 1,287,000 shares or $64,311,000.)

64,311,000 ÷ $636,582,000 = 10.1 %

C. INCOME ACCOUNT RATIOS

C-1. *Margin of Profit*

Operating income divided by net sales.

Formula: (4) ÷ (1)   or

$175,258,000 ÷ $1,362,995,000 = 12.8 %

Used to determine the operating efficiency, the ratio indicates that for every dollar of sales the company had 0.128 cents left after paying all costs of operations. From this amount (plus other income) must be paid bond interest, income taxes, and preferred and common dividends. The Bristol-Myers profit margin is well above the average.

C-2. *Earnings on Invested Capital*

Net income plus fixed charges divided by the sum of the bonds, preferred stock, common stock, capital surplus, and retained earnings.

Formula: (7) plus (6) ÷ the sum of (19) through (23) or

$116,883,000 ÷ $636,582,000 = 18.4 %

The percentage earned on total invested capital is the true test of the profitability of a business because it reflects not only the efficiency of the operation (margin of profit) but the way in which the enterprise is capitalized as well. The invested capital figure is that of the year-end. It is more customary to use average invested capital. This amount is the invested capital of the previous year averaged with that of the current year. The 1972 year-end invested capital of Bristol-Myers was $609,243,000. When averaged with the 1973 amount, the figure is $622,912,-000. The percentage earned on this amount was 18.8 %.

C-3. *Fixed Charge Coverage*

Total income divided by fixed charges.
Formula: (5) ÷ (6)   or
$$\$196,510,000 \div \$15,120,000 = 13.0 \text{ times}$$
Fixed charges were covered 13 times in 1973. The recommended standards require that fixed charges be covered 7 times in the most recent seven-year period or at least 5 times in the poorest of those seven years. Total income in the years 1967–1973 averaged $152,173,000, and in the poorest year—1967—it came to $109,979,000. In the main test the coverage came to 10 times, and in the poorest-year test it was 7.5 times. This coverage is ample.

C-4. *Preferred Dividend Coverage*

Total income divided by the sum of fixed charges and twice preferred dividends.
Formula: (5) ÷ (6) plus (2 × 8)   or
$$\$196,510,000 \div \$20,266,000 = 9.7 \text{ times}$$
The standards here are the same as for the fixed-charge coverage. For the seven-year period the coverage was 7.5 times, and in the poorest-year test it was 5.4 times. The preferred dividend has been well covered.

C-5. *Earnings per Share of Common Stock*

Balance for common divided by the number of shares of common stock outstanding.
Formula: (9) ÷ (21, expressed as shares)   or
$$\$99,190,000 \div 31,355,344 = \$3.16$$

C-6. *Effect of Dilution*

The company has $12.2 million of 4½ % debentures convertible into common stock at $57.50 per share. Also each preferred share is convertible into 0.53 shares of common. If these conversions were assumed in 1973, the earnings per share would not be reduced. Hence no adjustment of common earnings for dilution is required.

C-7. *Depreciation as a Percentage of Cost of Plant*

Formula: (3) ÷ (15)   or
$$\$20,175,000 \div \$369,082,000 = 5.5\%$$
The depreciation charge of 5.5 % is in line with the twenty-seven industry groups listed in Table 8. U.S. manufacturing corporations experience annual depreciation at rates ranging from 9.7 % to 4.2 % and averaging 6.2 % of gross plant. The annual report states that depreciation is charged on a straight-line basis.

C-8. *Depreciation as a Percentage of Net Sales*

This ratio is used, at times, in comparing companies within an industry.
Formula: (3) ÷ (1)   or
$$\$20,175,000 \div \$1,362,995,000 = 1.5\%$$
Depreciation as a percentage of net sales is below average. A more typical figure would be 3.2 %. Some but not all of the difference reflects the use of straight-line depreciation as opposed to accelerated depreciation.

C-9. *Common Stock Dividends as a Percentage of Earnings (Payout)*

Dividends paid on common stock divided by the balance for common stock.
Formula: (10) ÷ (9)   or
$$\$40,424,000 \div \$99,190,000 = 41\%$$
The payout of earnings in the form of dividends was the same as that of the Dow-Jones Industrial Average ($35.33 ÷ $86.16) in 1973.

PART IV: Definitions of Financial
Terms and Phrases

N.B.: This list does not include most of the terms related to trading in securities—e.g., "uptick," "short sale," "wire-house," etc. These terms are defined in a booklet—*The Language of Investing* —obtainable on request from member firms of the New York Stock Exchange.

ACCELERATED AMORTIZATION—Extra-rapid depreciation (usually in a five-year period) allowed on facilities constructed for war or defense purposes.

ACCELERATION CLAUSE—Provision in a bond indenture whereby the principal may be declared due in advance of maturity because of default in payment of interest or some other "event of default."

ACCRUALS—Expenses charged against current operations but not requiring cash payment therefor until some future date. Thus bond interest may be accrued on the corporation's books each month, although it usually is paid only at six-month intervals. Accruals may also refer to credit items, such as interest accrued on securities held.

ACCUMULATIVE (DIVIDENDS)—Same as CUMULATIVE.

ADJUSTMENT BONDS—See INCOME BONDS.

"AFTER ACQUIRED PROPERTY" CLAUSE—A provision in a mortgage indenture which places property subsequently acquired by the issuing company under the lien of the mortgage.

AMORTIZATION—The process of gradually extinguishing a liability, deferred charge, or capital expenditure over a period of time. Thus: (1) a mortgage is amortized by periodically paying off part of the face amount; (2) bond discount is amortized by periodically charging the earnings of each year during which the bonds are outstanding with their proper share of the total discount; (3) fixed assets are amortized by charges for depreciation, depletion, and obsolescence.

ARBITRAGE—Simultaneous completion of purchase and sale of securities (or commodities) at a profit-yielding price spread, made possible by: (1) existence of trading in such security or commodity in more than one marketplace; or (2) by existence of two separate securities with established terms of exchange from one to the other. *Example of* (1): simultaneous sale in the London market and purchase in New York of United States Steel at a spread sufficient to provide expenses plus a profit. *Example of* (2): simultaneous sale in the same marketplace of a common stock and the purchase of a bond or preferred stock currently convertible at a definite ratio into such stock, or of "rights" entitling the owner upon payment of a fixed amount of cash to acquire such stock, the spread in prices being sufficient to provide expenses plus a profit. Most arbitrage now takes place in connection with a pending plan of merger, acquisition, or reorganization by purchase of a security and sale of another (or others) into which it will be exchanged under the plan, at prices indicating a net profit if and when the plan is effective; or merely by holding the purchased security for receipt of a cash payment which will exceed the cost.

ARTICLES OF ASSOCIATION—A document similar to a charter or certificate of incorporation setting forth the terms under which an enterprise is authorized by the state to do business.

ASSET VALUE—The same as definition (2) of BOOK VALUE.

ASSETS—The resources, properties, money, claims, etc. owned by a corporation. See CAPITAL ASSETS, CURRENT ASSETS, DEFERRED ASSETS, INTANGIBLE ASSETS, and TANGIBLE ASSETS.

AUDIT—An examination of the financial status and operations of an enterprise, based mostly on the books of account, and undertaken to secure information for, or to check the accuracy of, the enterprise's balance sheet, income statement, and/or surplus statement. See also CERTIFIED REPORT.

BALANCE SHEET—A report of the financial status of an enterprise on a specific date. It lists in one column all the assets owned and their values, and in another column the claims of creditors and the equity of the owners. The two columns are always equal in total amount.

BASIS—In the case of bonds, the yield to maturity at a given price, as shown by the bond tables.

BILLS PAYABLE—Technically, unconditional orders in writing upon the enterprise by another enterprise or person for the payment of a sum of money. In practice they usually represent bank loans payable.

BLUE CHIP ISSUES—A colloquial term applied to stocks which are of accepted investment merit and are popular market leaders. These generally sell at a higher than average ratio of price to current earnings and dividends.

"BLUE SKY" FLOTATIONS—Originally applied to promotions of companies whose securities have no value. So named because the purchaser receives no more than "blue sky" for his money. State and federal laws to prevent such flotations are now in force. Registration of securities under such state laws is now called "blue-skying."

BOND—A certificate of debt which: (1) represents a part of a loan to a business corporation or governmental unit, (2) bears interest, and (3) matures on a stated future date. Infrequently a bond issue may fail to possess one of these characteristics. Short-term bonds (generally running for five years or less from date of issuance) are often called notes.

BOND DISCOUNT—In financial statements, represents the excess of face value of a bond issue over the net amount received therefor by the issuing corporation. This discount usually is amortized over the life of the bonds. In popular investment parlance, represents the excess of the face value of a bond over its current market price. A bond "selling at a discount" is one selling at a price less than 100, or par. Conversely, a bond "selling at a premium" is at a price above par.

BONDS, STRAIGHT—Bond conforming to the standard pattern, i.e., (1) unqualified right to repayment of a fixed principal amount on a fixed date, (2) unqualified right to fixed interest payment on fixed dates, (3) no further interest in assets or profits and no voice in the management.

BONDS, UNDERLYING—Bonds which have precedence over some other bond or bonds. They usually hold a first mortgage on property of a corporation which is also pledged under a junior general mortgage.

BOOK VALUE—(1) Of an asset: the value at which it is carried on the company's books. (2) Of a stock or bond issue: the value of the assets available for that issue, as stated on the books, after deducting all prior liabilities. It is generally stated at so much per share or so much per $1,000 bond. The accepted practice excludes intangibles in computing book value, which is thus the same as "tangible asset value," "net asset value," or equity per share.

BREAK-UP VALUE—In the case of an investment fund or a holding company issue, the value of the assets available for the issue, taking all marketable securities at their market price.

BUSINESSMAN'S INVESTMENT—An investment in which a certain amount of risk is recognized but is thought to be offset either by the chance of increased principal value or by a high income return. (In our view, the second consideration is generally unsound.) This term is based on the thought that a businessman is both financially able to assume some risk and capable of following his investments intelligently.

CALLABLE FEATURE—A provision of a bond issue by which it may be retired in advance of maturity at the option of the company, not the holder. The feature may provide for various prices at various times. Also applies to preferred stock.

CALLS—See PUTS AND CALLS.

CAPITAL (OF A BUSINESS)—(1) In the narrower sense, the dollar value assigned in the balance sheet to the various stock issues. (2) In a broader sense, the investment represented by the stock issues and the surplus. (3) In a still broader sense, the same as the foregoing but adding thereto all long-term obligations. See CAPITALIZATION.

CAPITAL ASSETS OR FIXED ASSETS—Assets of a relatively permanent nature which are held for use or income rather than for sale or direct conversion into salable goods or cash. The chief capital assets are real estate, buildings, and equipment, often referred to together as "plant account" or "property account." Intangible assets, such as good will, patents, etc., are also capital assets.

CAPITAL EXPENDITURES—Expenditures or outlays of cash or its equivalent which are undertaken to increase or improve capital assets.

CAPITAL GAIN—Under tax law, a gain realized on the sale of securities, fixed property, or similar assets. If the asset has been held more than six months it is long-term gain and the income tax thereon is not more than one-half that on ordinary income.

CAPITAL GAIN DIVIDEND—A dividend paid by a regulated investment company out of its long-term capital gains. Such dividends are treated by the recipient, for federal tax, as the equivalent of long-term capital gains of their own.

CAPITAL STRUCTURE—The division of the capitalization as between bonds, preferred stock, and common stock. Where common stock represents all or nearly all the capitalization, the structure may be called "conservative"; where common stock represents a small percentage of the total, the structure is called "speculative."

CAPITAL SURPLUS—See SURPLUS.

CAPITALIZATION—The aggregate of the various securities issued by a corporation, including bonds, preferred stock, and common stock. (It is sometimes a question of judgment whether a short-term obligation should be considered part of the capitalization or a noncapital current liability. If it falls due within a year, it is usually considered to be a current liability.)

CAPITALIZING EXPENDITURES—Certain kinds of expenditures may

at the option of the company be treated either as current expense or capital expense. In the latter case the expenditure appears on the balance sheet as an asset, which is generally written off gradually over a period of years. Examples of such expenditures: intangible drilling costs of oil concerns, development expense of mines, research and development (R&D) expense of manufacturing companies, organization expense, expense of floating bond and stock issues, etc. In many such cases the full amounts are deducted immediately for income tax purposes but they are capitalized (and then gradually written off) in the reports to stockholders.

CAPITALIZING FIXED CHARGES—Computing the principal amount of a debt which would carry the fixed charges in question. Method: divide the fixed charges by the assumed interest rate. *Example:* fixed charges of $100,000, capitalized at 8%, yield a principal value of $1,250,000.

CASH ASSET VALUE—The value of the cash assets (cash and cash equivalents) alone applicable to a given security issue, after deducting all prior liabilities. Ordinarily stated at so much per share or per $1,000 bond. The cash asset value of a stock is sometimes stated without deducting liabilities from the cash assets. This should be termed the "gross cash asset value," and it is a useful calculation only when the other assets exceed all prior liabilities. In the latter case it may be called the "free-cash" asset value.

CASH EQUIVALENTS—Assets held in place of cash and convertible into cash within a short time. *Examples:* time deposits, U.S. government bonds, and other marketable securities.

CASH FLOW—See discussion in Chapter 30 (page 67).

CERTIFICATE OF DEPOSIT—(1) A receipt for a security deposited with a protective committee or other agency for some purpose such as a reorganization plan. These certificates of deposit, known as c/d's, are generally transferable and are dealt in as securities. (2) The same as a time deposit.

CERTIFICATE OF NECESSITY—A document issued by the government entitling a company to charge accelerated amortization against a specified percentage of the cost of a new facility related to war or defense.

CERTIFIED REPORT—A corporate report (balance sheet, income statement, and/or surplus statement), the correctness of which is attested to by a certified public accountant as the result of an independent audit. In a thorough study it is advisable to look carefully at the accountant's certificate appended to the report, since audits vary widely as to their scope, and a given audit may be subject to important limitations and reservations.

CHARTER—The certificate of incorporation or franchise received from the state, legally authorizing the corporation to carry on business as set forth under the grant of powers in the charter.

CIVIL LOANS—Loans contracted by a government agency—national, state, or municipal.

CLASS A STOCK—A name given to a stock issue to distinguish it from some other stock issue of the same company, generally called Class B or merely common. The difference may lie in voting rights, dividend or asset preferences, or other special dividend provisions. If there is a preference, it is generally held by the Class A shares, but other advantages may go either to the Class A issue or to the other common stock issue.

CLOSED-END INVESTMENT COMPANY—An investment fund which does not offer new shares continuously nor undertake to redeem shares on demand. Thus its capital remains relatively fixed, but its shares may sell in the open market at a varying percentage of the applicable net asset value.

COLLATERAL TRUST BONDS—Bonds secured by other securities (either stocks or bonds) deposited with a trustee. The real investment merit of these bonds depends upon either or both of (1) the financial responsibility of the company issuing them, and (2) the value of the deposited securities.

CONSOLIDATED STATEMENT—A corporate report (balance sheet, income statement, and/or surplus statement) that combines the separate statements of the corporation and its subsidiaries and sometimes controlled enterprises. Such consolidated reports eliminate all intercompany accounts, and show the entire group of companies as if it were a single enterprise. Sometimes only 100 %-owned subsidiaries are included; often foreign subsidiaries are excluded as well as finance companies controlled by a manufacturing enterprise.

CONSOLIDATION—A combination of two or more companies into one, to form a new company. See MERGER.

CONTINGENCY RESERVES—Reserves set up out of earnings or surplus to indicate a possible future loss or claim against the corporation, the likelihood of which is open to considerable question (e.g., possible future decline in the market value of inventories or marketable securities owned). In most cases they may be regarded as part of the surplus, but occasionally indicate *probable* as well as merely possible losses or claims. These were formerly in common use but now are rarely found in financial statements.

CONTINGENT LIABILITIES—Liabilities indefinite as to either their amount or their occurrence. *Examples:* amounts involved in law suits or tax claims; liabilities under a guarantee.

CONTROLLED COMPANY—A company whose policies are controlled by another through ownership of 51 % or more of its voting stock. (A lower percentage may carry effective control or working control.)

CONVERSION PARITY OR CONVERSION LEVEL—That price of the common stock which is equivalent to a given quotation for a convertible issue, or vice versa. For example, if a preferred stock is convertible into 3 shares of common stock and sells at 90, the conversion parity for the common would be 30. If the common is selling at 25, the conversion parity for the preferred would be 75. This may also be called the *conversion value* of the preferred stock.

CONVERSION PRICE—That price of the common stock equivalent to a price of 100 for a convertible bond or a convertible preferred stock of $100 par value. For example, if a $1,000 bond is convertible into 40 shares of common stock, the conversion price of the common is $25 a share.

CONVERSION PRIVILEGE—See CONVERTIBLE ISSUES.

CONVERTIBLE ISSUES—Bonds or preferred shares which are convertible into other securities at a prescribed price or ratio *at the option of the holder.* Usually convertible into the common stock of the corporation, but sometimes bonds are convertible into preferred stock or even into other bonds. The holder is in the position of a creditor or senior stockholder of the corporation with the privilege of additional profits if the enterprise prospers.

CREDIT—(1) A company's borrowing capacity, in terms of amount and interest costs, as determined by its overall financial standing. (2) a bookkeeping entry. See DEBIT & CREDIT.

CUMULATIVE DEDUCTIONS METHOD—A method of computing bond interest coverage which takes into account only the interest on bonds of prior or equal rank to the issue being considered. Interest on bonds of junior rank is ignored by this method. This method should be used, if at all, only as a secondary test, supplementing the overall method. See OVERALL METHOD.

CUMULATIVE PREFERRED STOCK OR INCOME BOND—A preferred stock carrying dividends—or an income bond carrying interest— at a fixed rate and entitled to receive all such dividends or interest not paid in previous years before the common stock can receive any payment. Some issues are cumulative only to the extent that dividends and interest have been earned but unpaid in any year. (Suggested title for these: earned cumulative issues.) In the case of many railroad income bonds the accumulation of interest is limited (usually to a maximum of three years), after which they become noncumulative.

CUMULATIVE VOTING—An arrangement whereby each share of stock may cast as many votes for one director as there are directors to be elected. Its effect is to permit a substantial minority to elect one or more directors. Mandatory in twenty-one states and permitted in seventeen others; in the latter it must be specified in the bylaws of the corporation. In addition, cumulative voting is required by federal statute for all national banks.

CURRENT ASSET VALUE—The value of the current assets alone applicable to a given security, after deducting all prior liabilities. Ordinarily stated as so much per share or so much per $1,000 bond.

CURRENT ASSETS—Assets which either are cash or can be readily turned into cash or will be converted into cash fairly rapidly in the normal course of business. Include cash, cash equivalents, receivables due within one year, and inventories. (Slow-moving inventory should properly be excluded from current assets, but it is not customary to do so.)

CURRENT LIABILITIES—Recognized claims against the enterprise which are considered to be payable within one year.

DEBENTURES—Obligations of a corporation secured only by the general credit of the corporation. Have no direct lien on specific property of the corporation. (Sometimes applied, with no special meaning, to a preferred stock issue.)

DEBIT & CREDIT—Bookkeeping terms to describe types of accounts and entries to accounts.

DEED OF TRUST—See INDENTURE.

DEFENSIVE INVESTMENT—An investment policy which places its chief emphasis on minimizing both the risk of (eventual) loss and the need for special knowledge, skill, and continuous attention. See ENTERPRISING INVESTOR.

DEFERRED ASSETS, OF DEFERRED CHARGES—Bookkeeping assets representing certain kinds of outlays which will eventually be treated as expenses. They are not immediately charged to any expense account because they are more properly chargeable against future years' operations. Include unamortized bond discount, organization expense, development expense, and prepaid advertising, insurance, and rent. These latter prepaid expenses are sometimes called prepaid assets, and the portion applicable to the next twelve months may be included in current assets.

DEFERRED MAINTENANCE—The amount of repairs that should

have been made to keep plant in good running condition, but that have been put off to some future time. This measure of equipment neglect usually does not appear in the corporate reports, although its existence frequently is suggested by maintenance expenditures drastically lower than those of earlier years. This is most readily noticeable in the income accounts of railroads.

DEFICIT—When appearing in the balance sheet, represents the amount by which assets fall short of equaling the sum of liabilities (creditors' claims) and capital stock. When appearing in the income statement, usually represents the amount by which revenues fell short of equaling expenses and charges. An "operating deficit" means a loss *before* deducting fixed charges. "Deficit after dividends" is self-explanatory.

DEPLETION—The reduction in the value of a wasting asset due to the removal of part of that asset, e.g., through mining ore reserves or cutting timber.

DEPLETION RESERVE—The valuation reserve reflecting the total depletion to date of the assets to which it pertains (usually mineral or timber resources). Deduction of this reserve from the corresponding balance sheet asset indicates the corporation's valuation (generally its unamortized cost) of what remains of the asset, i.e., its net value.

DEPRECIATION—The loss in value of a capital asset, due to wear and tear or obsolescence that cannot be compensated for by ordinary repairs. The purpose of the bookkeeping charge for depreciation is to write off the original cost of an asset (less expected salvage value) by equitably distributed charges against operations over its entire useful life. (When in any year more is charged on the books for depreciation than is reinvested in plant, the excess may be called "unexpended depreciation.")

DEPRECIATION RESERVE—The valuation reserve reflecting the total book depreciation to date, and therefore indicating the expired portion of the useful life of the assets to which it pertains. A depreciation reserve of $200,000 against a $1,000,000 asset indicates not that the asset's present resale value is $800,000, but rather that about 20 % of the asset's useful life is believed to have expired.

DEVELOPMENT EXPENSE—(1) The cost of developing, manufacturing or other processes or products to make them commercially usable. New enterprises frequently treat such items as deferred assets; established and successful enterprises more frequently treat them as current expense. It is now customary to speak of research and development expense (R&D) together. (2) The cost of opening up an oil or mining property—in most cases treated as a deferred asset.

DILUTION—(1) From the standpoint of a convertible issue, an increase in the number of common shares without a corresponding increase in the company's assets. Most convertible issues are protected against this contingency by an "antidilution clause," which reduces the conversion price in the event of dilution. (2) The adverse effect on the earnings per share of common stock resulting from the existence of convertible securities.

DIVERSIFICATION—Spreading the risk of investment by dividing the funds to be invested among a number of issues. An investment fund may diversify among different industries; or—less effectively—among different companies in the same industry; or geographically. Applies also to the kinds of business carried on.

DIVIDEND COVERAGE—The number of times a dividend has been earned in a given period. Preferred dividend coverage should properly be stated only as the number of times the combined fixed charges and preferred dividends have been earned. Common dividend coverage is stated separately, but the figure must be viewed in the light of the senior obligations.

DIVIDEND SCRIP—(1) Certificates issued as a scrip dividend (see SCRIP DIVIDENDS). (2) Fractional shares of stock received as a stock dividend. These fractional shares usually are not entitled to dividends or voting power until combined into full shares.

DIVIDEND YIELD—A percentage figure, found by dividing the dividend rate in dollars by the market price in dollars. Example:

If a stock paying $4 annually sells at $80, the dividend yield is: $4/80 = 5.00\%$.

DIVISIONAL LIENS—A term usually applied to bonds secured by a mortgage on a section of minor length of a railroad system. If the mileage covered by the lien is a valuable part of the system, the specific security is good. If the mileage covered by the lien is of small value to the system the specific security is poor.

DOLLAR COST AVERAGING—An investment program under which the same dollar amount is placed in one or more common stocks at fixed successive intervals—e.g., quarterly or annually—over a good many years. The result is to build up the investor's common stock portfolio at an average cost per share somewhat below the actual average price for the period, since he acquires more shares at the lower levels than at the higher. This policy prevents the common error of concentrating stock buying during periods of high share prices.

EARNED SURPLUS—See SURPLUS.

EARNING POWER—Properly, a rate of earnings which is considered as "normal," or reasonably probable, for the company or particular security. It should be based both upon the past record and upon a reasonable assurance that the future will not be vastly different from the past. Hence companies with highly variable records or especially uncertain futures may not logically be thought of as having a well-defined earning power. However, the term is often loosely used to refer to the average earnings over any given period, or even to the *current* earnings rate.

EARNINGS RATE—The annual earnings stated as so much per share, or (less frequently) as a percentage of the par value.

EARNINGS RATIO—See PRICE-EARNINGS RATIO.

EARNINGS YIELD—The ratio of the market price to the annual earnings. *Example:* A stock earning $6 annually and selling at 50 shows an earnings yield of 12%. See also PRICE-EARNINGS RATIO.

EFFECTIVE DEBT—The total debt of a company, including the principal value of annual lease or other payments which are equivalent to interest charges. (Such may not appear as part of the funded debt.) The effective debt may be calculated by capitalizing fixed charges (see definition) at an appropriate rate. Where long-term bond issues carry an abnormally high or an abnormally low coupon rate, the effective debt may be thought of as higher or lower than the face value.

EFFECTIVE PAR—In the case of preferred stocks, the par value which would ordinarily correspond to a given rate of dividend. Found by capitalizing the dividend in dollars at an appropriate rate, say, 8 %. *Example:* The effective par of a $2.40 preferred stock would be 2.40/0.08 = 30. Useful when dealing with no par preferred issues or those having a par out of line with the dividend rate.

ENTERPRISING (OR AGGRESSIVE) INVESTOR—One who follows a policy aimed at combining a sufficient degree of safety with a better than average return. For success it requires a special degree of knowledge, skill, and attention. See DEFENSIVE INVESTMENT.

EQUIPMENT OBLIGATIONS OR EQUIPMENT TRUST CERTIFICATES—Bonds, usually maturing serially, secured by a lien on the rolling stock of a railroad. There are two methods generally used to protect the creditor: (1) the Philadelphia Plan, now almost universal (title to equipment rests in hands of trustees until all certificates have been paid off, at which time title is transferred to the corporation); (2) the New York Plan (a conditional bill of sale is given to the corporation which issues the certificates; after the certificates have been paid off the corporation receives unqualified title).

EQUIPMENT RENTALS—Sums paid by one railroad to another railroad or to other owners of specialized equipment for the use of rolling stock. These payments are on a per diem (per day) basis, in accordance with a standard schedule. The amounts paid or received appear in the railroad income statement immediately after the tax item.

EQUIPMENT TRUST—An arrangement relating to the ownership

or control of equipment (usually rolling stock of railroads) by a trustee, under which equipment trust certificates or bonds are issued. Often used to mean equipment trust certificates.

EQUITY—The interest of the stockholders in a company, as measured by the capital and surplus. Also the protection afforded a senior issue by reason of the existence of a junior investment.

EQUITY METHOD—A presentation of the income account and the balance sheet which shows the proportionate interest of the company in the profits and the net assets of partially owned affiliates.

EQUITY SECURITIES—(1) Any stock issue, whether preferred or common. (2) More specifically, a common stock or any issue equivalent thereto through having a virtually unlimited interest in the assets and earnings of the company (after prior claims, if any).

EQUITY, TRADING ON THE—When a businessman borrows money for his business, to supplement his own capital, he is said to be "trading on the equity." The underlying idea is that more profit can be made on the borrowed capital than the interest paid thereon. The phrase is sometimes used to mean specifically the extreme case where most of the capital is borrowed and only a small amount is owned.

EXPENDITURES VS. EXPENSES—Expenditures are outlays of cash or the equivalent; frequently they involve no concurrent charge against operations or earnings (e.g., capital expenditures). Expenses are costs, i.e., charges against current operations or earnings; frequently they involve no concurrent cash expenditures (e.g., accruals, depreciation).

FACTOR OF SAFETY—A method of stating fixed charge coverage, as the percentage of the balance after fixed charges to the fixed charges. *Example:* earnings available for interest, $175,000; interest charge $100,000. Factor of safety equals

$$\frac{175,000 - 100,000}{100,000} = 75\%$$

Factor of safety equals (interest coverage − 1) × 100 %. (This term is becoming obsolete.)

FIFO (FIRST-IN, FIRST-OUT)—The usual way of determining cost of inventory on hand. Sales are deemed to be made against the earliest acquired items; hence inventory remaining represents those latest acquired. See LIFO.

FISCAL YEAR—The twelve-month period selected by a corporation as the basis for computing and reporting profits. Usually coincides with the calendar year (i.e., ends December 31) but often differs from it. Many merchandising companies' fiscal year ends January 31, to facilitate inventory-taking after the close of the most active season; while some meatpackers' fiscal year ends October 31, for the same reason.

FIXED ASSETS—See CAPITAL ASSETS.

FIXED CHARGES—Interest charges and other deductions equivalent thereto. These include rentals, guaranteed dividends, subsidiary preferred dividends ranking ahead of parent company charges, and amortization of bond discount (the annual allowance to write off discount on bonds sold). Ordinarily, building rents are not considered fixed charges, but are included in operating expenses.

FLOATING ASSETS—Same as CURRENT ASSETS.

FLUSH PRODUCTION—In the oil industry, the large production yielded by new oil wells during the first period of their life. This lasts a short time and is succeeded by a "settled production" at a much smaller rate. In analysis it is important not to consider the earnings from flush production as permanent.

FORECLOSURE—The legal process of enforcing payment of a debt secured by a mortgage, by selling the properties and distributing the proceeds to the lien holders. This may be done when the principal or interest on the mortgage is not paid.

FORMULA-INVESTING PLAN—A method of investment which determines mechanically the dates and amounts of purchases and sales of common stock on a "true investment" as opposed to a speculative or trading basis. It generally provides for purchases at fixed rates as the market declines and for sales (of shares owned) at fixed rates as the market advances. There are many varieties of such plans. Dollar cost averaging (which see) is a special type of formula-investment plan since it depends only on time intervals and does not provide for any sales.

FUNDED DEBT—Debt represented by securities, i.e., by formal written agreements evidencing the borrower's obligation to pay a specified amount at a specified time and place, with interest at a specified rate. Includes bonds, debentures, and notes, but does not include bank loans.

GOING-CONCERN VALUE—The value of an enterprise considered as an operating business, and therefore based on its earning power and prospects rather than on liquidation of its assets.

GOLD CLAUSE—A clause in virtually all bonds issued for many years prior to 1933, under which payment was promised in gold dollars of the same weight and fineness as existed when the debt was contracted. No longer legal since 1933.

GOOD WILL—Intangible asset purporting to reflect the capitalization of excess future profits expected to accrue as a result of some special intangible advantage held, such as brand names, reputation, or strategic location. In practice, the amount at which good will is carried on the balance sheet is rarely an accurate measure of its true value. Now usually carried at $1, except for "purchased good will" (which see. See also INTANGIBLE ASSETS).

GROSS INCOME—Sometimes used as the equivalent of gross sales. More often represents an intermediate figure between gross sales and net income.

GROSS REVENUES OR GROSS SALES—Total business done, without deduction of costs or expenses.

GROWTH STOCK—A common stock which has shown a faster than average rate of increase in earnings in the past and is expected to enjoy this advantage in the future. Some authorities would say that a true growth stock must be expected to double its per share earnings in not more than ten years—i.e., it must grow at an average rate of not less than 7.2 % per year.

GUARANTEED ISSUES—Bonds or stocks which are guaranteed as to principal, interest, dividends, sinking fund, etc., by a company other than the issuer. Guarantees usually come about through lease of the property of the issuing company to another company, or to facilitate the sale of securities by one company which is controlled by another. The value of the guarantee depends upon the credit standing and earnings of the guaranteeing company; but a guaranteed issue may stand on its own feet, even though the guarantee itself is questionable.

HEDGE—(1) Usually, to make a commitment in commodities for future delivery, in order to avoid risk of price change in such commodity entering into the cost of goods already contracted for manufacture and sale. (2) In stock market operations, to purchase a senior convertible issue and sell short the amount of common stock obtainable if the conversion privilege is exercised (or other operations similar thereto). (3) More recently, an investment program involving simultaneous purchases and sales of unrelated common stocks. (HEDGE FUNDS.)

HOLDING COMPANY—A corporation which owns all or a majority of the stock of subsidiaries. The distinction sometimes made between a *holding company* and a *parent company* is that the latter is an operating company which also owns or controls other operating companies, whereas the holding company merely holds or controls operating companies.

HOUSE OF ISSUE—Investment banking company engaged in underwriting and distribution of security issues.

IDLE-PLANT EXPENSE—The cost of carrying (maintaining and allowing for depreciation on) nonoperating manufacturing properties.

INCOME ACCOUNT—A report of operations over a specified period of time, summarizing the revenues or income and the expenses or costs attributed to that period, and indicating the net profit or loss for the period. Frequently called the *profit & loss statement*.

INCOME BONDS—Bonds whose interest payments are dependent on

earnings. In some bonds part of the interest is on a fixed basis, and the balance is on an income or contingent basis. Income bonds are sometimes called adjustment bonds.

INDENTURE—The legal document prepared in connection with a bond issue, setting forth the terms of the issue, its specific security, remedies in case of default, duties of the trustee, etc. Also called the "deed of trust."

INTANGIBLE ASSETS—Capital (fixed) assets which are neither physical nor financial in character. Include patents, trademarks, copyrights, franchises, good will, leaseholds, and such deferred charges as unamortized bond discount. These assets should be shown on the balance sheet at cost, if at all, but frequently are assigned purely arbitrary values. Good will now appears mostly as the cost of an acquired business in excess of its net tangible assets; in many cases such cost is charged off against earnings (amortized) over a period of about 10 years.

INTERCORPORATE DEBT—Debt of one corporation to another corporation controlling it, controlled by it, or controlled by the same interests that control the debtor.

INTEREST COVERAGE—The number of times that interest charges are earned, found by dividing the (total) fixed charges into the earnings available for such charges (either before or after deducting income taxes).

INTRINSIC VALUE—The "real value" behind a security issue, as contrasted with its market price or book value. Generally a rather indefinite concept; but sometimes the balance sheet and earnings record supply dependable evidence that the intrinsic value is substantially higher or lower than the market price.

INVENTORIES—Current assets representing the present stock of finished merchandise, goods in process of manufacture, raw materials used in manufacture, and sometimes miscellaneous supplies such as packing and shipping material. Usually stated at cost or market value, whichever is lower. (See FIFO and LIFO).

INVESTMENT COMPANY—The official name given to an enterprise

which invests its capital in a varied list of securities, intending to give its bond and stockholders the benefit of expert financial management and diversification. Formerly (and still often) called an investment trust. A good unofficial term is "investment fund." See CLOSED-END INVESTMENT COMPANY, OPEN-END INVESTMENT COMPANY, and MUTUAL FUND.

JOINT FACILITY RENTS—In railroad income statements, represent rentals paid (dr) or received (cr) for terminal facilities or other similar properties used jointly by several railroads.

JOINT AND SEVERAL GUARANTEE—A guarantee by more than one party under which each party is potentially liable for the full amount involved if his associates do not meet their share of the obligation.

JUNIOR ISSUE—An issue whose claim for interest or dividends, or for principal value, comes after some other issue, called senior issue. Second mortgages are junior to first mortgages on the same property; common stock is junior to preferred stock; etc.

LEASEHOLD—The right to occupy a property at a specified rental for a specified period of years. To obtain a long-term lease at a favorable rental a cash bonus may be paid by the lessee to the lessor (owner), if it is a new lease, or to the former lessee, if the lease is taken over. The balance-sheet item "leaseholds" should represent only this cash consideration, and should be amortized over the life of the lease.

LEASEHOLD IMPROVEMENTS—The cost of improvements or betterments to property leased for a period of years. Such improvements ordinarily become the property of the lessor (owner) on expiration of the lease; consequently their cost must be amortized over the life of the lease.

LEASEHOLD OBLIGATIONS—The obligation or liability, inherent in a leasehold, to pay a specified rental for a specified period of years.

LEGAL INVESTMENTS—Securities which conform with the regulations set up by legislative enactment governing the investments made by savings banks and trust funds in a given state. Usually, the banking department of the state publishes annually a list of securities (commonly referred to as "legals") considered eligible for investment by savings banks and trust funds.

LEVERAGE—The condition making for wide changes in per share earnings and market value, arising from the fact that a company's common stock has relatively heavy fixed costs or deductions (interest and/or preferred dividends) ahead of it. Small percentage changes in gross earnings or operating costs, or total asset values in the case of investment funds, will affect the earnings and market price of the common stock in much greater ratio. A leverage stock usually sells at a small aggregate figure in proportion to the total amount of senior securities.

LIABILITIES—Recognized claims against an enterprise. In its common and narrower sense includes only creditors' claims, i.e., excludes the claims of owners represented by the capital stock, surplus, and proprietorship reserve accounts. In its broader sense includes all items on the right side of the balance sheet.

LIABILITY RESERVE—A reserve or claim against an enterprise representing a liability the existence of which is unquestioned but the exact amount of which cannot as yet be determined (e.g., loss reserves of an insurance company).

LIFO (LAST-IN, FIRST-OUT)—A method of valuing inventory on hand intended to minimize inventory profits and losses. Sales are deemed to be made against the most recently acquired items. Hence inventory remaining represents those earliest acquired. (See FIFO.) The dollar amount of an inventory on LIFO is almost always lower than it would be on FIFO.

LIQUID ASSETS—Same as current assets; but sometimes applied to current assets excluding inventory (quick assets).

LIQUIDATING VALUE—The amount which would be available for a security if the business were wound up and the assets turned into cash. Is usually less than book value, because allowance must be made for shrinkage in the value of the various kinds of assets if sold during a short period.

LOADING CHARGE OR SALES LOAD—The premium above net asset

value, generally from 6 to 9 %, charged by open-end investment funds on the sale of new shares, to cover selling costs. It is incorrectly stated by the funds as a percent of the (marked-up) selling price.

MAINTENANCE—Upkeep and repair costs required to maintain plant and equipment in efficient operating condition.

MARGIN OF PROFIT—Operating income divided by sales. Depreciation is usually included in the operating expense, while income taxes are usually excluded. Nonoperating income received and interest charges paid are not included in arriving at the operating income.

MARGIN OF SAFETY—In general the same as interest coverage, which appears above. See FACTOR OF SAFETY. Formerly used in a special sense, to mean the ratio of the balance after interest to the earnings available for interest. The preferable term is now FACTOR OF SAFETY.

MARKETABILITY—The facility with which a security may be bought and sold. Good marketability requires a continuous close relation between bid and offering prices sufficient to permit ready purchase or sale in fair volume. Sometimes called liquidity.

MERGER—A combination in which one company absorbs one or more other companies.

MINORITY INTEREST—In a consolidated income statement, represents the interest or equity of the minority stockholders of a subsidiary in the earnings of that subsidiary. In a consolidated balance sheet, represents the interest or equity of these minority stockholders in the net worth of the subsidiary.

MORTGAGE, "BLANKET"—Usually the same as general mortgage. May be applied more specifically to a mortgage issue covering a number of separate properties.

MORTGAGE, GENERAL—A lien on all the fixed property of a corporation at the time of issuance, usually junior to underlying mortgages.

MORTGAGE, GUARANTEED—A mortgage on real estate on which payment of principal or interest (usually both) is guaranteed by a mortgage guarantee company or a surety company. Sometimes the whole mortgage is sold with the guarantee attached; frequently one or more mortgages are deposited with the trustee, and "guaranteed mortgage certificates" are issued with the mortgage(s) as security.

MUTUAL FUND—An open-end investment company.

NEGOTIABLE INSTRUMENTS—Certain kinds of property, e.g., currency, checks, promissory notes, acceptances, coupon bonds, title to which passes on delivery and cannot be attacked when in the hands of a holder in due course and in good faith. Stocks are not negotiable instruments; hence stolen certificates may be recovered from an innocent holder.

NET CURRENT ASSETS (WORKING CAPITAL)—Current assets less current liabilities.

NET PLANT—See PROPERTY ACCOUNT.

NET QUICK ASSETS—Either same as net current assets or (preferably) net current assets excluding inventory.

NET WORTH—The amount available for the stockholders preferred and common, as shown by the books. Is made up of capital, surplus, and such reserves as are equivalent to surplus. It is ordinarily used to include intangible assets as they appear on the books, and to that extent differs from the book value or net asset value of the stock issues.

NONCUMULATIVE PREFERRED STOCK—Preferred stock subject to the provision that if dividends are not declared in any period, the holder loses all rights to dividends for that period. Where the dividends are cumulative to the extent earned, the issue stands midway between a straight cumulative and a straight noncumulative preferred.

NONDETACHABLE WARRANTS—See WARRANTS.

NONRECURRENT ITEMS—Earnings or deductions from some special source not likely to appear in subsequent years. Such items should be separated from the regular earnings or deductions in analyzing a report. *Examples of nonrecurrent earnings:* profit on sales of capital assets; special dividends from nonconsolidated affiliates; profit on bond retirement; amount received in settlement of litigation; etc. *Examples of nonrecurrent deductions:* loss on sale of capital assets; special inventory write-off; idle plant expense (in some cases); etc.

OBSOLESCENCE—The loss of value of a capital asset resulting from new manufacturing developments or inventions which render the asset commercially unusable. Also, the accounting charge (usually part of the depreciation charge) to adjust for the probable future loss in value resulting from these causes.

OPEN-END INVESTMENT COMPANY—An investment fund which by charter provision agrees to redeem its shares at net asset value (or slightly less) on demand. Nearly all these funds sell additional shares continuously, in most cases at a premium ("loading charge") above the net asset value.

OPERATING RATIO—In the case of railroads, the ratio found by dividing total operating revenue (or gross revenue) into operating expenses excluding taxes. In the case of public utilities, it is generally defined as the ratio of operating expenses, including taxes and depreciation, to the total revenue. Similarly in the case of industrials, except that some authorities do not include depreciation and most do not include income taxes in operating expenses.

OPTION—See PUTS AND CALLS.

OPTION WARRANTS—See WARRANTS.

ORGANIZATION EXPENSE—Direct costs of forming a new corporate enterprise: mostly incorporation fees and taxes and legal fees. May appear on the balance sheet as a deferred asset; if so, is usually written off against the first few years' earnings.

OVERALL METHOD—The proper method of calculating bond interest or preferred dividend coverage. In the case of bond interest it means finding the number of times that *total fixed charges* are covered. In the case of preferred dividends it means finding the number of times that the aggregate of all *fixed charges plus preferred dividends* is covered. (In dealing with a preferred issue senior to another preferred issue, the requirements of the junior issue may be omitted.)

PAR, PARITY, PAR VALUE—For par value see discussion in Chapter 4. "Par" means 100 % of face value for a bond or preferred stock, and generally $100 per share for a common stock (regardless of its actual par value). "Parity" generally refers to the price of a convertible issue corresponding to the market or assumed price of the related common stock, and vice-versa.

PARENT COMPANY—See HOLDING COMPANY.

PARTICIPATING ISSUES—Bonds (very infrequently) or preferred stocks which are entitled to additional interest or dividends, above the regular rate, depending either on (1) the amount of earnings, or (2) the amount of dividends paid on the common stock.

PLANT ACCOUNT—See PROPERTY ACCOUNT.

PORTFOLIO—Refers to an investor's holdings of securities in terms of their distribution among bonds, preferred stocks, and common stocks, and among individual securities.

PRE-EMPTIVE RIGHT—The right of shareholders to purchase additional shares or other securities (generally securities convertible into common stock) before these are sold to other purchasers. Pre-emptive rights are generally accorded stockholders under state laws, but may be waived in the charter or bylaws.

PREFERRED STOCK—Stock which has prior claim on dividends (and/or assets in the case of dissolution of the corporation) up to a certain definite amount before the common stock is entitled to anything. See CUMULATIVE PREFERRED STOCK, NONCUMULATIVE PREFERRED STOCK, and PARTICIPATING ISSUES.

PREMIUM ON BONDS—The excess of the market price of a bond, or the amount received by the issuer, over its face value.

PREMIUM ON CAPITAL STOCK—The excess of cash or equivalent received by the issuer over the par value or stated value of capital stock issued therefor.

PREPAID ASSETS—See DEFERRED ASSETS.

PRICE-EARNINGS RATIO—Market price divided by current (or some other) annual earnings per share. *Example:* Stock selling at 84 and earning $7 per share has a price-earnings ratio of 12 to 1 (or is said to be selling at 12 times earnings).

PRIOR DEDUCTIONS METHOD—An entirely improper method of calculating bond interest or preferred dividend coverage. The requirements of senior obligations are first deducted from earnings and the balance is applied to the requirements of the junior issue. See OVERALL METHOD.

PRIOR LIEN—A lien or mortgage ranking ahead of some other lien. A prior lien need not itself be a first mortgage.

PRIOR PREFERRED—A preferred issue ranking ahead of another preferred issue of the same company.

PRIVILEGED ISSUE—A bond or preferred stock which has a conversion or participating right, or has a stock purchase warrant attached to it.

PROFIT & LOSS STATEMENT—See INCOME ACCOUNT.

PROFIT & LOSS SURPLUS—See SURPLUS.

PROPERTY ACCOUNT—The cost (or sometimes, the appraised value) of land, buildings, and equipment acquired to carry on business operations. *Net property account* represents cost or appraised value of these assets less accrued depreciation to date, i.e., property account less depreciation reserve. The terms *plant* and *net plant* frequently are used with the same respective meanings, but sometimes exclude land or nonstationary assets such as delivery equipment.

PROPRIETORSHIP RESERVES—Reserves set up as segregations of surplus, which serve merely to earmark part of the stockholders' equity as not subject to distribution in the form of cash dividends. Include most contingency reserves and also reserves for sinking funds and plant extensions. Represent not liabilities, but equities.

PROSPECTUS—A document describing a new security issue; especially, the detailed description which must be supplied to intending purchasers under the Securities Act of 1933.

PROTECTIVE COMMITTEE—A committee, generally organized at the initiative of substantial holders of a given security, to act for all the owners of that security in important matters in difficulty or dispute. Most protective committees arise in connection with a corporate trusteeship (receivership) and deal with the question of reorganization. Others may develop merely because of differences of opinion on some basic policy; e.g., between certain stockholders and the management.

PROTECTIVE COVENANTS—Provisions in a bond indenture, or charter provisions affecting a preferred stock, (1) which bind the company not to do certain things considered injurious to the issue or, (2) which set forth remedies in the event of unfavorable developments. *Example of* (1): agreement not to place a lien on the property ahead of the bond issue. *Example of* (2): the passing of voting power to the preferred stock if dividends are not paid.

PROXY—An authorization given by a security holder to someone else to vote his holdings for directors, or on some question put to vote.

PURCHASE MONEY MORTGAGES—Mortgages issued in partial payment for real estate or other property and having a lien on the property purchased. They are often used to circumvent the "after acquired property clause" in bonds which a company has previously issued.

"PURE INTEREST"—The theoretical interest rate on a riskless investment. Varies with general credit conditions. The actual interest rate on a given investment is presumed to be made up of the pure interest rate, plus a premium to measure the risk taken.

PUTS AND CALLS—A call is a right to buy (from the writer of the call) shares of stock at a stated price, expiring on a stated date. Similarly, a put is a right to sell shares at a stated price. These so-called options can be bought and sold in special markets. There are technical provisions relating to dividends, etc.

PYRAMIDING—In stock market operations, the practice of using unrealized paper profits in marginal trading to make additional purchases. In corporate finance, the practice of creating a speculative capital structure by a series of holding companies, whereby a relatively small amount of voting stock in the parent company controls a large (and usually heavily bonded) corporate system.

QUALITATIVE FACTORS (IN ANALYSIS)—Considerations which cannot be stated in figures, such as management, strategic position, labor conditions, prospects, etc.

QUANTITATIVE FACTORS (IN ANALYSIS)—Considerations which can be stated in figures, such as balance sheet position, earnings record, dividend rate, capitalization setup, production statistics, etc.

QUICK ASSETS—Sometimes (1) used to mean current assets, but (2) preferably, current assets excluding inventory.

RECEIVERSHIP—Operation of a company by an agent of the court, under direction of the court, usually arising from inability to meet obligations as they mature. There are technical differences between (1) an equity receivership, (2) a bankruptcy receivership, and (3) a trusteeship under Section 77 and Chapter 10 of the Bankruptcy Act.

RED-HERRING PROSPECTUS—A preliminary prospectus for information purposes, so-called because each page contains a large red legend warning that the document is not final or binding.

REGISTRATION STATEMENT—The forms filed by a corporation (or foreign governmental body) with the Securities and Exchange Commission in connection with an offering of new securities or the listing (registration) of outstanding securities on a national securities exchange. The prospectus, supplied to intending purchasers of a new issue, contains most, but not all, of the information given in the registration statement.

REGULATED INVESTMENT COMPANY—Under the tax law (Internal Revenue Code) an investment fund which can avoid income tax on its ordinary income and capital gains by distributing these profits as dividends and by meeting various other statutory requirements. See CAPITAL GAIN DIVIDEND.

RESERVES—Offsets against total or specific asset values, set up on the books (1) to reduce or revalue assets, (2) to indicate the existence of liabilities, generally of uncertain amount, or (3) to earmark part of surplus for some future use. See VALUATION RESERVES, LIABILITY RESERVE, and PROPRIETORSHIP RESERVES. Properly speaking, reserves represent not assets, but claims against or deductions from assets. Assets (usually cash equivalents) set aside to take care of reserves should be called reserve *funds*.

RESTRICTED SHARES—(1) Common stock issued under an unusual agreement whereby they do not rank for dividends until some event has happened—usually the reaching of a certain level of earnings. (2) Shares that may not be sold except under specified conditions.

RETIREMENT EXPENSE—In the income account or balance sheet an accounting charge in lieu of depreciation to provide for retirement of plant items expected generally in the near future. It was formerly used by public utility companies with the purpose and result of understating the true depreciation charges and overstating the reported earnings. No longer permitted by regulatory authorities.

RIGHT—A privilege accorded to the holder of each unit of an existing security to purchase new securities. Generally rights must be exercised within a short time, and the new security is offered at a price under the existing market. See WARRANTS.

ROYALTY—A payment made (1) for the use of a patent, (2) to the owner of oil or gas lands by those extracting oil or gas therefrom, or (3) to the author of a book, play, etc.

SCRIP DIVIDENDS—Dividends payable in notes or other written promises to pay the amount involved in cash at a later date. The date may be fixed, or contingent on certain happenings, or entirely discretionary with the directors.

SEASONAL VARIATIONS OR FLUCTUATIONS—Changes in operating results due to the time of the year. Allowance must be made for these in interpreting the results shown over part of the year.

SEASONED ISSUES—Securities of established large companies which have been favorably known to the investment public for a period of years covering good times and bad.

SECULAR TREND—A long-term movement, e.g., of prices, production, etc., in some definite direction. Opposed to seasonal fluctuations or variations.

SEGREGATION—Separation from a holding or operating company of one or more of its subsidiaries or operating divisions, effected by distributing stock of the subsidiary to the shareholders of the parent company.

SENIOR ISSUE—See JUNIOR ISSUE.

SERIAL BONDS—A bond issue providing that certain portions thereof mature on successive dates instead of all at once. Serial maturities are usually spaced one year apart. Nearly all railroad equipment obligations are serial issues.

SINKING FUND—An arrangement under which a portion of a bond or preferred stock issue is retired periodically in advance of its fixed maturity. The company may either purchase a stipulated quantity of the issue itself, or supply funds to a trustee or agent for that purpose. Retirement may be made by call at a fixed price, or by inviting tenders, or by purchase in the open market. The amount of the sinking fund may be fixed in dollars, or as a percentage of the issue, or based upon volume of production or earnings.

SLIDING-SCALE PRIVILEGE—A conversion or stock purchase privilege in which the price changes (almost always unfavorably to the senior issue) either with the passage of time or upon exercise of the privilege by a given amount of the issue.

SPECIAL SITUATION—An indicated security purchase that is expected to show an attractive profit because of some corporate development—such as sale of the company, reorganization, etc. —which is largely independent of the general movement of security prices.

SPECULATION—Financial transactions involving acknowledged risk entered into with the purpose of profiting from anticipated future events.

SPLIT-UP—Division of a corporation's share capital into a greater number of share units, usually (in the case of shares having a par value) by reduction in the par value represented by each share. Thus a split-up might consist of issuance, in exchange for each share of $100 par common stock outstanding, of four new $25 par common shares. Sometimes the reverse procedure is resorted to, i.e., the share capital is consolidated into a fewer number of shares by issuing only a fraction of a new share in exchange for each old share outstanding. For lack of a better title, this is frequently referred to as a *reverse split* or *split-down*.

STATED VALUE (OF CAPITAL STOCK)—Value at which no-par capital stock is carried on the balance sheet. May be a purely arbitrary or nominal amount. (In some states, par value shares may be given a stated value less than their par.)

STOCK DIVIDENDS—Dividends payable in the form of stock of the declaring company, but not necessarily of the same class as the shares receiving the stock dividend. (Infrequently, a stock dividend is paid in shares of a company other than the declarer, but this should rather be called a "distribution in kind.")

STOCK PURCHASE WARRANT—See WARRANTS.

STOCK-VALUE RATIO—(1) In the case of a bond, the ratio of the total market value of the capital stock of a corporation to the par value of its funded debt. (2) In the case of a preferred stock, the ratio of the total market value of the common stock issues to the total par value of all the bonds plus the total market value of the preferred stock.

STRAIGHT INVESTMENT—A bond or preferred stock, definitely limited in interest or dividend rate, purchased solely for its income return and without reference to possible increase in value.

SUBSIDIARY—A company controlled by another company (called the parent company) through ownership of at least a majority of its voting stock.

SURPLUS—The excess of the total net worth or stockholders' equity over the total of par or stated value of the capital stock and the amount of proprietorship reserves. At least part of this excess usually results from earnings retained in the business. This part frequently is labeled *earned surplus* or *profit & loss surplus* to indicate its source. That part of surplus arising from other sources (e.g., write-ups of fixed asset values, write-downs of the par or stated value of capital stock issues, or sale of stock at a premium) frequently is labeled *capital surplus.*

SURPLUS STATEMENT—A financial report summarizing the changes in surplus during the fiscal year (or other period). Shows surplus at beginning of period, plus net income for the period, less dividends declared, plus or minus any extraordinary credits to or charges against surplus. Final item of report, consequently, is surplus at end of period. Report also called *statement of surplus* and *analysis of surplus.*

SWITCHING—The process of selling a presently owned security and replacing it by another to gain some expected advantage.

TANGIBLE ASSETS—Assets either physical or financial in character, e.g., plant, inventory, cash receivables, investments. See INTANGIBLE ASSETS.

TAX-EXEMPT BONDS—Obligations of a state or a subdivision (e.g., a municipality), interest on which is not subject to federal income tax. Such issues are generally free of state income tax in the state of issuance but not elsewhere.

TIME DEPOSIT—Money on deposit with a bank withdrawable at the end of a (short) period instead of on demand, and generally drawing interest.

TREASURY STOCK—Lawfully issued stock that has been reacquired by the corporation through purchase or donation.

TREND—A persistent change (e.g., of earnings) in a certain direction over a given period. Caution must be used in projecting a past earnings trend into the future.

TRUSTEE—(1) One to whom the title to property has been conveyed for the benefit of another party. Thus the trustee for a mortgage bond issue holds the mortgage (i.e., has conveyed to it the mortgage property) for the benefit, primarily, of the bondholders. The trustee in bankruptcy holds title to the bankrupt's property (with certain exceptions) for the benefit primarily of the bankrupt's creditors. (2) A trustee may also assume obligations not connected with the direct holding of property, e.g., a trustee under the indenture of an unsecured (debenture) bond, or a person exercising voting rights under a voting trust.

TRUST FUND—Funds held by a trustee for the benefit of another. Terms set forth by the creator of the trust govern the type of property in which the trustee may invest, whether restricted to "legal investments" or left to the discretion of the trustee.

UNAMORTIZED BOND DISCOUNT—That part of the original bond discount which has not yet been amortized, or charged off against earnings.

UNDERLYING BONDS—See BONDS, UNDERLYING.

UNEXPENDED DEPRECIATION—See DEPRECIATION.

VALUATION RESERVES—Reserves set up (1) to indicate a diminution in present value of the assets to which they pertain, or (2) to provide for a reasonably probable failure to realize full value. *Example of* (1): depreciation and depletion reserves, reserve to reduce securities owned to market value. *Example of* (2): reserve for bad accounts.

VOTING TRUST—An arrangement by which stockholders turn over their voting rights (generally for directors only) to a small group of individuals called voting trustees. The original stock certificates are registered in the name of the voting trustees and held in trust, the stockholders receiving instead other certificates called "voting trust certificates" (abbreviation v.t.c.). Voting trusts generally run for five years. They usually give the v.t.c. holders all the privileges of the deposited securities, except that of voting.

WARRANTS—(1) Stock purchase warrants or option warrants. A right to purchase shares of stock, generally running for a longer period of time than the ordinary subscription rights given shareholders. These warrants are often attached to other securities, but they may be issued separately or detached after issuance. Nondetachable warrants cannot be dealt in separately from the security with which they were issued, and can be exercised only upon presentation with the original security. Option warrants are often issued in reorganizations or granted to management as additional compensation and incentive. (2) A name given to certain kinds of municipal obligations.

WASTING ASSETS—Tangible fixed assets subject to depletion through gradual removal in the normal course of operations of the business (e.g., metal, oil, or sulfur deposits; timberlands).

WHEN ISSUED—A term applied to dealings in securities proposed to be issued under some reorganization, merger, or new capitalization scheme. The full descriptive phrase is "when, as, and if issued." If the plan is abandoned, or changed materially, the "when issued" trades are void.

WORKING CAPITAL—The net current assets. Found by deducting current liabilities from the current assets.

WORKING CONTROL—Ownership of a substantial portion of the voting shares of a company (but less than 50% plus) sufficient to give control of the enterprise because the remaining shares are held by scattered owners.

YIELD—The return on an investment, expressed as a percentage of cost. *Straight yield* or *current yield* is found by dividing the market price into the dividend rate in dollars (for stocks) or interest rate (for bonds). It ignores the factor of maturity or possible call at a price higher or lower than the market. *Amortized yield* or *yield to maturity* (of a bond) takes into account the eventual gain or loss of principal value to be realized through repayment at maturity. Where a bond is callable before maturity, the amortized yield might be lower if it is assumed that call takes place. The true amortized yield should be the lowest shown on any assumption as to call.